HBCU

STEM Pathways

HBCU

STEM
Pathways

MYCHAL WYNN

VOL III: WHY ATTEND AN HBCU SERIES

HBCU STEM Pathways

Vol III: Why Attend an HBCU series

ISBN 13: 978-1-880463-57-4

Printing 1

For information about special discounts for bulk purchases, contact Rising Sun Publishing Special Sales at 1.770.518.0369 or via email at info@rspublishing.com.

For information about booking the author, Mychal Wynn, to speak to students, or to provide training for teachers, parents, counselors, coaches, and school staff, contact Rising Sun Publishing Speaking and Training Department at 1.770.518.0369 or via email at info@rspublishing.com.

Rising Sun Publishing is the exclusive publisher for the Foundation for Ensuring Access and Equity, Inc., a Marietta, Georgia Community-based Organization whose mission is to expand college access for underserved, under-resourced, first generation, and marginalized youth.

Mychal-David Wynn, Editor
David Escobar, Cover Design

RISING SUN
PUBLISHING
P.O. Box 70906
Marietta, GA 30007
(770) 518-3069
E-mail: info@rspublishing.com
Website: www.rspublishing.com

Printed in the United States of America.

Acknowledgments

I would like to acknowledge my wife, Nina, who has committed herself and joined me in my efforts over the course of many years, to expand the college and scholarship outcomes of students from throughout the United States. Between the many prayers, prayed on behalf of students and families, and the thousands of text messages exchanged with students and parents, she has availed herself 24/7 to help others.

I would like to acknowledge my good friend, and retired California Community College professor, Dr. Karen McCord, who is a relentless advocate for students. It was her phone call inviting me to support the California Community Colleges Guaranteed HBCU Transfer Pathways that was the catalyst for the *Why Attend an HBCU* series of books.

I would also like to thank my son and editor, Mychal-David Wynn, who has a BA in English from Amherst College and who has committed his literary expertise to not only supporting our work, but editing essays of hundreds of students to ensure they present their best writing in their college and scholarship applications.

Dedication

This book is dedicated to those who are advocating for equity and opportunity—the founding principal of Historically Black Colleges and Universities.

Give someone a fish, and you feed them for a day.
Teach someone to fish, and you feed them for a lifetime.

Table of Contents

Foreword

Most students are aware that the acronym STEM stands for Science, Technology, Engineering, and Mathematics, however, few students have been introduced to the range of careers that fall within each of these categories. Healthcare careers, which also fall under the broad category of STEM, are addressed separately in *Vol II* of this series, *HBCU Healthcare Pathways*. In that book, The National Center for Health Workforce Analysis, *"State of the U.S. Health Care Workforce, 2023,"* profiles the underrepresentation of Blacks in the healthcare workforce where Blacks represent only:

- 13.7% of Nurses
- 5.3% of Physician Assistants
- 4.1% of Dentists
- 4.1% of Physical Therapists
- 2.7% of Chiropractors
- 1.9% of Pharmacists
- 1.5% of Veterinarians

Similarly, the National Center for Science and Engineering Statistics' 2023 report, *"Diversity and STEM: Women, Minorities, and Persons with Disabilities,"* profiles the underrepresentation of Blacks across the science, technology, engineering, and mathematics workforce where Blacks represent only:

- 9% of Scientists & Engineers
- 6% of Social and Related Scientists
- 6% of Computer and Mathematical Scientists
- 4% of Biological, Agricultural, and other Life Scientists
- 4% of Physical and Related Scientists

Whether you are reading this book because you are considering a college major in STEM or exploring potential careers in STEM, this book will provide insight into both the obstacles and opportunities through HBCUs into graduate school or into the workforce. Whatever obstacles experienced by students in K-12 schools, HBCUs have a history of successfully preparing Black students for careers in STEM. Dr. Claudia Rankins, Program Director at the National Science Foundation, in "*Historically Black Colleges and Universities (HBCUs): NSF's Role in Building Capacity for STEM Education and Research*," reports that while HBCUs only enroll 9% of Black undergraduate students, they graduate:

- 29.9% of Black students in Agriculture
- 27.8% of Black students in Physical Science
- 25.5% of Black students in Mathematics
- 24.7% of Black students in Biological Sciences
- 17.2% of Black students in Engineering

The underrepresentation of Blacks in STEM careers has far reaching implications for families and communities. Rakesh Kochhar and Mohamad Moslimani in "*Wealth gaps across racial and ethnic groups*," note the huge gaps in wealth and homeownership between racial groups.

Average Household Wealth by Racial Group:

- Asians - $320,900
- Whites - $250,400
- Hispanics - $48,700
- Black - $27,100

Percentage of Home Ownership by Racial Group:

- 70% of Whites own their home
- 58% of Asians own their home
- 47% of Hispanics own their home
- 40% of Blacks own their home

Increasing household wealth and expanding homeownership can be profoundly impacted by attaining an undergraduate degree in virtually any STEM career. The Georgetown University report, "*The College Payoff: Education, Occupations, Lifetime Earnings*," (Carnevale, Rose, & Cheah, 2011) estimates lifetime earnings for an undergraduate degree is between $2 million and $4 million in all of the following STEM careers:

- $4 million - Pharmacists
- $3.9 million - Aircraft Pilots & Air Traffic Controllers
- $3.7 million - Computer & Information Systems Managers
- $3.6 million - Software Engineers
- $3 million$^+$ - All Engineers
- $3 million - Computer Scientists & Programmers
- $2.8 million - Architects
- $2.5 million - Registered Nurses
- $2.3 million - Agricultural, Biological, and Life Scientists

Whether or not you believe that a career in STEM is the right career for you, this book will provide guidance in exploring these careers, salaries for these careers, level of education required for these careers, the type of college curriculum associated with these careers, HBCUs considered leaders in preparing students for these careers, and how to match your interests to potential career pathways.

A Student's Perspective—Sydnee B.

As an eighteen year old high school student, I was unaware of how I would pay for my college education and pursue my goals of becoming a Physical Therapist. As a triplet, paying for 3 children entering college at the same time, would have placed a huge financial burden on my parents. It was not until Mr. and Mrs. Wynn urged me to explore HBCUs and apply for the Lewis and Elizabeth Dowdy Scholarship at North Carolina A&T State University that my path became clear and my parents' financial burden would be lessened.

Prior to applying to an HBCU, I had no prior knowledge of the many merit-based full ride scholarships offered by NC A&T and other HBCUs, like the full scholarship that one of my sisters received from Claflin University. However, Mr. and Mrs. Wynn urged me to research these programs, informed me of the Dowdy scholarship, guided me throughout my application process, and prepared me for the scholarship interview. While in high school, I was a varsity basketball player for both my high school and AAU teams and was committed to developing a deep understanding of bodily movement, exercise, and nutrition. After receiving my acceptance letter to North Carolina A&T, I was excited about the experiences that I anticipated gaining by attending an HBCU on my pathway toward becoming a physical therapist. Over my four years of participating in the kinesiology program at NC A&T, I have been impressed by the growth and development the program has undergone, the leadership and professional experience that I have gained, and the quality of education that I have received.

Having little prior knowledge about HBCUs, I have been surprised by many things. The curriculum is pertinent and relevant to every aspect of my undergraduate preparation. Many of my professors were not only teaching the most recent information on biomechanics, neuromuscular connection, nutrition and exercise physiology, but were also conducting their own on-campus research. I was able to serve as a research assistant from freshman year throughout my time at NC A&T. I cannot overly express the incredible opportunity of applying the knowledge I was learning in class, supporting a professor's research, presenting papers at conferences, and networking with professors and healthcare professionals. Engaging in research at such an early stage in my college career opened doors for more research, employment, and mentoring opportunities.

I have received tremendous support throughout my undergraduate years to enhance my professional readiness and been exposed to a plethora of opportunities to develop a deep understanding of the field of kinesiology. The academic requirements, mandatory classes, internship courses, experiences outside of class, and support in preparation for applying to graduate school have all been part of the HBCU *culture of caring*. As I reflect on the many career oriented activities, internship opportunities, alumni events, career fairs, and graduate school displays, I am taken aback at just how much support has been offered and opportunities to which I have been exposed.

As I reflect on my 4 years at North Carolina A&T, I also reflect on the college planning guidance and support that enabled me to attend NC A&T on a full scholarship. Not only did my family and I avoid large sums of student loan debt, I was able to finance a majority of my graduate school application fees through my scholarship. In addition to the hugely beneficial financial support, my scholarship offered many networking and professional development opportunities. Events such as leadership retreats and alumni panels, not only helped me to grow, but seeing how other Dowdy Scholars were engaging in their respective fields provided invaluable experiences and a sense of pride in the totality of the HBCU experience.

For future STEM majors seeking advice on where to start on their journey, I would recommend a few things:

- Do extensive research and know why you want to pursue a particular major or program of study.
- Contact the dean or director of your program and inquire about details such as number of full time faculty, professional opportunities and additional resources for students in your major, as well as common student complaints and how the program is working to address them.

- If you envision continuing your education into graduate school, then research graduate school programs now, in the same manner in which you are researching your undergraduate program (e.g., scholarships, admissions criteria, etc.). I admittedly did not research early acceptance/early assurance programs into Doctor of Physical Therapy (DPT) programs so I definitely advise you to do so if this is your desired career pathway.
- The college planning guidance that I received as a high school student in building my résumé, helped me to become a competitive college and scholarship applicant. So, by maintaining a detailed list of every activity, including my community service hours, throughout my undergraduate experience, I have been able to transition my high school résumé into a curriculum vitae, which now supports my research, internship, and graduate school applications.

Finally, as a STEM major, you may compare yourself to others, experience burnout from an intense curriculum, and struggle with maintaining a healthy work-life balance. It is important to prioritize your mental health and wellness. This process can be difficult to navigate alone, so lean into the resources offered by your school, friends, professors, and classmates. Needless to say, while you may leave your family to attend college, you should always cling to the love and support offered by your family. Do not be afraid to ask for help! Building healthy coping mechanisms can help ensure that you can continue to be a successful student and professional.

Sydnee Brothers
North Carolina A&T State University, Class of 2025
Lewis and Elizabeth Dowdy Scholar
Candidate for a BS in Kinesiology
Department of Kinesiology

Note: Sydnee is a triplet. She, together with each of her sisters, all received full scholarships (Claflin University, North Carolina A&T State University, and Wesleyan University)

From the Author

Many of the issues confronting students pursuing educational and career pathways today are similar to the experiences encountered in my journey over 50 years ago as a high school student attending Chicago's DuSable High School. While I was generally a good student with long-term aspirations, I attended a high school with one of the lowest graduation rates in America, where only 25 percent of students graduated and less than 5% went on to attend a 4-year college or university. Neither of my parents graduated from high school. They were part of *The Great Migration* of Blacks from Memphis, Tennessee to northern cities in search of jobs and opportunity. My father dropped out of school at the end of 8th grade and eventually hopped a freight train to Chicago. My mother dropped out of school at the end of 10th grade and took a segregated Greyhound Bus to Chicago. My journey to Chicago was even more unconventional. I was born in Pike County, Alabama at home to a single-parent mother in what would have been referred to as a "shotgun shack." Born to a mother too poor to care for yet another child, I was given up for adoption before my first birthday. I was taken aboard a segregated bus to Sharon, Pennsylvania where my biological father's sister arranged to have me adopted by a friend who lived in Chicago.

In my journey through the Chicago Public Schools, interrupted by a brief period in grades 6 through 10, where I attended Catholic school, I cannot recall receiving any college planning guidance whatsoever from a counselor or through my school. As a high school senior, I attended my first college fair as a photographer for my high school yearbook. While I was taking pictures, a Black representative from Northeastern University— the only Black college representative that I encountered—invited me to his table and told me about the Northeastern University Cooperative Education Program and the opportunity to work my way through college. Knowing nothing about financial aid or scholarships, I left that fortuitous encounter with my only guidance about applying to college and applied directly and solely to the Northeastern

University College of Engineering.

After several months, I received a letter from Northeastern. It was a *conditional acceptance*—conditional on my passing classes in physics and calculus, subjects not offered at my high school. I accepted the conditions and in the fall, following my high school graduation, I attended Chicago's Kennedy-King Community College, now part of the City Colleges of Chicago, where I earned an 'A' in physics and a 'B' in calculus. Then, in a snow-covered winter, I boarded my first airplane, flew to Boston's Logan Airport, and enrolled in Northeastern University.

It was not long after enrolling at Northeastern that I discovered just how inadequately prepared I was to major in engineering. During my first two quarters, I failed nearly every class. Depressed and despondent, I was prepared to return home when I refused to be defeated. I reasoned that if I could survive the gangs and violence of growing up in Chicago, I could survive my college coursework. I changed my major from electrical engineering to business and computer science, which changed my whole orientation toward school. I excelled in my classes, earned my way onto the Dean's List, landed a co-op job with Accenture, a Global Business Consulting Firm, went on to graduate *honors cum laude*, and was recruited by companies from Boston to San Francisco. I accepted a job with IBM (a Global Business and Computing Company) at their Santa Teresa Research Laboratory in San Jose, California, as a Systems Design Software Engineer. My first year salary was more than my father had ever earned in his 30 years of driving long haul trucks for the U.S. Postal Service.

Whether you want to pursue a career pathway directly into the workforce after high school or through college; or into the military by enlisting immediately after high school or being commissioned after graduating from college, I hope to provide guidance towards choosing a pathway based on your gifts, talents, interests, and aspirations. Perhaps reading this book will be your fortuitous encounter.

Mychal Wynn

Introduction

A career pathway through a high school STEM (Science, Technology, Engineering, and Mathematics) program whether directly into the workforce or through college would be into what is forecast to be the largest growing and most highly paying occupations between 2022 to 2032.

The following table projects the top 15 fastest growing occupations and salaries—all of which are STEM occupations—from 2023 to 2033 based on information from the U.S. Bureau of Labor Statistics: Occupational Outlook Handbook, *"Fastest Growing Occupations."*

Occupation	**Median Salary**
Computer and Information Research Scientists	$145,080
Software Developers	$132,270
Physician Assistants	$130,020
Nurse Practitioners	$126,260
Information Security Analysts	$120,360
Actuaries	$120,000
Medical and Health Services Managers	$110,680
Data Scientists	$108,020
Mathematicians and Statisticians	$104,110
Operations Research Analysts	$83,640
Epidemiologists	$81,390
Occupational Therapy Assistants	$67,010
Physical Therapist Assistants	$64,080
Wind Turbine Service Technicians	$61,770
Solar Photovoltaic Installers	$48,800

The underrepresentation of Blacks in STEM and the top 15 jobs of the future being in STEM-related careers, provides incentive for colleges and employers to attract more Blacks into STEM majors and onto a trajectory into STEM careers to increase diversity and fill the jobs of the future. This incentive is supported by scholarships offered by colleges, governmental agencies, nonprofits, and private employers. Consequently, STEM pathways through HBCUs can lead to more scholarship opportunities, expanded workplace opportunities, higher long term earnings potential, and closing the household wealth gap between Blacks and other racial groups.

The U.S. Bureau of Labor Statistics Occupational Outlook Handbook provides career and salary data for many STEM-related occupations. Each of the following tables reflects job and salary data taken from each STEM occupational category.

Science Occupations[1]	**Median Salary**
Agricultural and Food Scientists	$76,400
Anthropologists and Archaeologists	$63,800
Atmospheric Scientists & Meteorologists	$92,860
Biochemists and Biophysicists	$107,460
Chemists and Materials Scientists	$87,180
Conservation Scientists and Foresters	$68,300
Economists	$115,730
Environmental Scientists and Specialists	$78,980
Epidemiologists	$81,390
Geographers	$90,880
Geoscientists	$92,580
Historians	$72,890
Hydrologists	$88,770
Medical Scientists	$100,890
Microbiologists	$85,470
Physicists and Astronomers	$149,530
Political Scientists	$132,350
Psychologists	$92,740
Sociologists	$101,770
Urban and Regional Planners	$81,800
Zoologists and Wildlife Biologists	$70,600

The Department of Family and Consumer Sciences (FCS) is one of the oldest programs at North Carolina A&T State University. It is the only comprehensive family and consumer sciences unit on the campus of a land-grant university in North Carolina and is one of three programs in the state that is accredited by the American Association of Family and Consumer Sciences. Following is the North Carolina A&T State University curriculum for food and nutritional scientists:

- Physics: 3 credits
- Agriculture: 3 credits
- Occupational Safety: 3 credits
- English: 6 credits
- Electives: 8 credits
- Biology: 8 credits
- Math (including Calculus): 11 credits
- Chemistry: 21 credits
- Food Science: 57 credits

Computer and Information Technology Occupations[2]	**Median Salary**
Computer/Information Research Scientists	$145,080
Computer Network Architects	$129,840
Computer Programmers	$99,700
Computer Systems Analysts	$103,800
Database Administrators and Architects	$117,450
Information Security Analysts	$120,360
Network/Computer Systems Administrators	$95,360
Software Developers	$130,160
Web Developers and Digital Designers	$92,750

South Carolina State University is designated as a Center of Excellence in Cyber Defense by the National Security Agency (NSA) and Department of Homeland Security (DHS). Following is the South Carolina State University 128-credit cybersecurity curriculum in computer science:

- Physics: 8 credits
- English: 9 credits
- Electives: 9 credits

- Math (including Calculus I, II): 20 credits
- Computer Science: 65 credits

Architecture and Engineering Occupations[3]	**Median Salary**
Aerospace Engineers	$130,720
Agricultural Engineers	$93,310
Bioengineers and Biomedical Engineers	$100,730
Chemical Engineers	$112,100
Civil Engineers	$95,830
Computer Hardware Engineers	$138,080
Drafters	$62,530
Electrical and Electronics Engineers	$109,010
Environmental Engineers	$100,090
Health and Safety Engineers	$103,690
Industrial Engineers	$99,380
Landscape Architects	$79,320
Marine Engineers and Naval Architects	$100,270
Materials Engineers	$104,100
Mechanical Engineers	$99,510
Mining and Geological Engineers	$100,640
Nuclear Engineers	$125,460
Petroleum Engineers	$135,690
Surveyors	$68,540

Tuskegee University stresses fundamentals of engineering science and analysis and the development of creative thinking in the application of the principles of engineering design. Laboratory work is concerned with experimental procedures in the field of solid mechanics, fluid mechanics, and heat transfer. Emphasis is given to technical reports and to their content, form, and presentation. Increasing emphasis is placed on computer application at all levels. Following is the Tuskegee University curriculum for mechanical engineering:

- Chemistry: 5 credits
- Physics: 8 credits
- English: 9 credits

- Electives: 14 credits
- Math (including Calculus I, II, III): 15 credits
- Engineering: 80 credits

Math Occupations[4]	**Median Salary**
Actuaries	$120,000
Data Scientists	$108,020
Mathematicians and Statisticians	$104,860
Operations Research Analysts	$83,640

At Howard University, students majoring in applied mathematics are required to minor in computer science, economics, biology, chemistry, physics, or business. Following is the Howard University 120-credit curriculum for applied mathematics:

- Philosophy: 3 credits
- English: 6 credits
- Computer Science: 7 credits
- Foreign Language: 14 credits
- Electives and Other Required Classes: 40 credits
- Math (including Calculus I, II, III): 50 credits

The more you learn about the career pathways and college majors most aligned with your interests, personality, temperament, and gifts and talents, the more capable you will be in focusing your college research. For example, the Quantum Insider article, "*7 Highest Paying Quantum Computing Jobs [+Average Salary]*" (Swayne 2022) provides insight into career pathways in this field:

- Quantum Physicists [$120,000+]
- Quantum Computer Scientists [$100,000+]
- Quantum Cryptography Scientists [$120,000+]
- Quantum Computing Software Engineers [$105,000+]
- Quantum Developers [$90,000+]

- Quantum Software Specialists [$90,000+]
- Quantum Engineers [$90,000+]
- Entry with bachelor's degree in physics, computer science, or electrical engineering.

If your interests align with the field of Quantum Information Sciences and Engineering, you might consider Howard University or any of the 23-affiliated HBCUs that are part of the IBM-HBCU Quantum Center at Howard University.

If your interests align with Artificial Intelligence, you might consider Prairie View A&M University or Alabama A&M University, which have received grants from the National Science Foundation and U.S. Army to expand their research in Artificial Intelligence.

There are expansive opportunities to align your interests with STEM pathways through HBCUs:

- Self-driving automobiles at North Carolina A&T State University.
- Video game management and design at Benedict College and Johnson C. Smith University.
- Flight Education at Delaware State University, Elizabeth City State University, Florida Memorial University, Hampton University, University of Maryland Eastern Shore, or Texas Southern University.
- Hampton University and Elizabeth City State University are partners with the Delta Airlines Propel College Pilot Career Path Program.
- Air Traffic Controller pathways through the FAA HBCU Initiative provides internship and career opportunities in partnership with 11 HBCUs.

As you explore the array of STEM pathways presented in this book, consider first and foremost, pursuing a college major and career trajectory that you will enjoy.

Obstacles or Opportunities?

If, as a Black student, you have earned top grades and test scores, particularly in math and science, you will have many college and scholarship opportunities. Beyond the obvious reason of simply being a top student, you will have distinguished yourself among students within your racial group. Statistically, the majority of Black college-going students are not graduating from high school adequately prepared for college majors in STEM. Amongst the many obstacles could be the student, the school, the teacher, or circumstances completely beyond the student's control. Whatever the reasons, the reality is: any Black student who has overcome such obstacles to become a top student with top test scores will discover an abundance of educational and scholarship opportunities at HBCUs. Even those students who are academically or financially challenged will have opportunities at HBCUs, which have a rich history of helping students rise above both academic and financial challenges, and providing students with academic support and scholarship opportunities.

Obstacle #1: Lack of exposure

The first obstacle to be overcome is the lack of exposure to the multitude of career opportunities in STEM. The 2024 Black Students and STEM Report, *"From Classroom to Careers,"* notes the gaps between aptitude, exposure, and career aspirations of Black students pursuing STEM career pathways:

- 75% of Black students lack exposure to such careers as industrial engineers, electrical engineers, mechatronics engineers, machinists, and manufacturing technicians.
- 57% of Black students lack exposure to such careers as physicians, pharmacists, laboratory technicians, nurses, dentists, and nutritionists.

- 53% of Black students lack exposure to such careers as architects, construction managers, electricians, facility managers, plumbers and pipefitters, cost estimators, and interior designers.
- 51% of Black students lack exposure to such careers as computer programmers, software developers, information systems engineers, cyber security analysts, and aerospace engineers.

The report also notes that despite having the aptitude, there is a disconnect between aptitude and career interest among Black female students:

- There is an 88% gap between aptitude and interest in Advanced Manufacturing.
- There is a 73% gap between aptitude and interest in Computers and Technology.
- There is a 72% gap between aptitude and interest in Architecture & Construction.

Joie, currently attending the Honors College at Spelman College discusses how she found her way onto a STEM pathway in one of her college essays:

> *"I had a ninth-grade project to research 'pandemic-proof' jobs. While I learned that some of the most pandemic-proof jobs are in the federal government, real estate, and finance, I found jobs in information technology and computer science constantly recurring in my research. Not only were they recurring, within technology there were multiple, seemingly sustainable career pathways. My research inspired me to meet with my counselor and add the Introduction to Digital Technology class to my tenth-grade schedule. By my senior year, I was taking the third-year course—Advanced Cybersecurity—and had two years of internship experience in IT and was firmly onto a STEM career pathway."*

The impact of her ninth-grade project and the course schedule changes that she advocated for herself supported her application to the computer science program and being offered admission into the Honors Program at Spelman College and her selection as a CodeHouse Scholar, a program providing mentorship and a $20,000 per year scholarship opportunity for students attending one of five HBCUs.

Like Joie, who went to her high school counselor and asked to be placed into the Introduction to Digital Technology class, Black students must advocate for themselves. Butrymowicz, Amy, & Fenn, in their Hechinger Report article, *"How career and technical education shuts out Black and Latino students from high-paying professions,"* note how easily Black students on a career pathway that does not align with their aptitude or interest:

> Kamara, who is Black, was enrolled in an "audio engineering" course that taught her how to make music tracks and videos instead of a regular engineering course that she recalls was mostly filled with white students.
>
> When she asked an administrator at Mount Pleasant High School about this apparent disparity, she said she was told that the audio engineering course was created for "regular students."

The article goes on to note:

> A Hechinger Report/Associated Press analysis of CTE enrollment data from 40 states reveals deep racial disparities in who takes these career-oriented courses. Black and Latino students were often less likely than their white peers to enroll in science, technology, engineering and math (STEM), and information technology classes. Meanwhile, they were more likely to enroll in courses in hospitality and, in the case of Black students in particular, human services.

Obstacle #2: Lack of access

The next obstacle is the lack of access to higher-level classes, particularly in math and science. Brinkley and Ma, in their Associated Press article, *"Black and Latino students lack access to certified teachers and advanced classes,"* provide insight into why many academically qualified Black students are not on an appropriately rigorous math pathway to prepare for college-level coursework in STEM:

> America's Black and Latino students are at a disadvantage in nearly every measure of educational opportunity, with less access to advanced classes, counselors and even certified teachers, according to data released Wednesday by the U.S. Education Department.
>
> Compared with their white peers, students of color were more likely to be in schools that had security staff but no counselor.
>
> Black students represented 15% of all high school students, but they made up just 8% of students in Advanced Placement science and 6% in AP math. Latino students represented 27% of all high school students but made up 20% in AP science and 19% in AP math.
>
> At many schools with larger rates of minority students, taking advanced courses wasn't even an option. The number of courses in math, science and computer science was fewer at the 5,500 public high schools where Black and Latino students represented more than 75% of all students.
>
> In 35% of schools with high Black and Latino enrollment, calculus wasn't offered, while it was available at 54% of schools with low Black and Latino enrollment.

Obstacle #3: Lack of placement/enrollment

Even Black students attending school where they have access to higher level math and science coursework, are not enrolling in the classes or being placed into the classes. Patrick, Davis, and Socol, in their Ed Trust article, *"Why Are Black and Latino Students Shut Out of AP STEM Courses?"* note the disconnect between aspirations and opportunity:

> 2 in 5 Black and Latino students say they really enjoy STEM (science, technology, engineering, and math) courses and aspire to go to college, but less than 3 percent are enrolling in STEM courses. Many aspiring young Black and Latino students across the nation who show a love for science early on and express an interest in pursuing it as a career, want to discover something new, to make a difference, and to help their families

and their communities.

The Systemic causes for under-enrollment include:

1. Reliance of education leaders on a student's persistence or assumptions about their intelligence instead of addressing barriers that make it difficult for students to enroll
2. Reliance on single denominators of readiness, such as GPA and test scores

Obstacle #4: Lack of subject-area preparation

The lack of exposure and lack of access to higher-level math and science classes during high school results in inequitable preparation for pursuing college STEM majors. Melba Newsome, in her Hechinger Report article, *"Even as colleges pledge to improve, share of engineering and math graduates who are Black declines,"* shares some of the challenges that students face:

> Despite graduating in the top 5 percent of his class, Jarred Young struggled at the University of Maryland because his high school hadn't offered advanced math.
>
> "I was doing algebra I in high school when my friends who went to the magnet school were taking algebra II, trigonometry, and one was already doing pre-calculus," he said. "By the time I got to Maryland, I was already two steps behind in math."
>
> Young struggled, had to repeat classes, and took five years to graduate, with support from another program, the Center for Minorities in Science and Engineering. He went on to earn a doctorate in aerospace engineering and joined the Clark School of Engineering faculty. Without the help he got, he said, he could have easily become another STEM casualty.

While Jarred received the support that he needed to overcome his math deficiencies, Koroma, despite being academically capable, found herself unable to overcome the biases and microaggressions of pursuing a STEM major in an environment where she was culturally isolated.

> As a college junior studying bioengineering, Amida Koroma was a fixture on the dean's list at the University of Maryland. Yet Koroma, who is Black, said she felt as if many of her white peers dismissed her as less capable.
>
> "When we're working on group projects, they'll say things like, 'You can do the typing,' as opposed to getting into the nitty-gritty of how to build this robot," she said. "Sometimes it feels like I have to prove myself all over again."
>
> "A lot of people develop impostor syndrome." She said she was often the only Black student in her engineering classes. "It's, like, 'Do I even belong here?' I wear a hijab, and being a Black Muslim woman, it's like being minority on minority on minority." This semester, Amida changed her major to psychology.

The Education Trust report, *"Opportunities Denied: High-Achieving Black and Latino Students Lack Access to Advanced Math,"* (Baker, Morgan, & Wade, 2023) provides further insight into how all of these obstacles disadvantage Black students in preparing to major in STEM disciplines in college:

> A solid foundation in algebra, geometry, and trigonometry is the prerequisite for placement in higher-level math courses that lead to college opportunity. However, too often, it is not ability, but student characteristics (such as race, wealth, and privilege) and/or school-based resources (such as instructional resources, placement practices, school culture, and teacher and school counselor behavior) that contributes to the stratification of higher-level learning opportunities by race and income. As such, narratives that imply that placement in advanced math coursework is earned suggest that underserved students perpetuate their own inequitable learning experiences, rather than acknowledge that systemic injustices facilitate these inequities in educational opportunities. Such assumptions do not explain the vast disparities in course access for students who are equally brilliant, have demonstrated achievement, but come from lower socio-economic backgrounds or are Black or Latino.

Obstacle #5: Lack of test preparation

The classes that you take during high school, and the level to which you engage in these classes, will have a direct impact on your SAT and ACT scores. These scores have huge financial implications. Even if you have a GPA that ranks you at the top of your class, it is important that you recognize the huge disparity in test scores among Black SAT and ACT test takers. Despite the many colleges that have become test optional, SAT and ACT scores continue to have a huge impact on college access and merit-based scholarship opportunities.

The ACT Profile Report, "Graduating Class of 2023," notes:

- Only 8% of Black students met the college readiness benchmark in math
- Only 9% of Black students met the college readiness benchmark in science
- The average ACT Composite Score for Black students was a 15 (28th percentile)

Top ACT math and science scores for students pursuing STEM majors is 30+ (94th percentile). While HBCUs like Tuskegee University offer merit scholarships, the average ACT scores of Black students fall far short of meeting the requirements. The Tuskegee Distinguished Presidential Scholarship requires a 3.7 unweighted GPA and an SAT score of 1300+ (86th percentile) or an ACT Composite score of 28+ (90th percentile). Additionally, STEM scholarships, dual degree programs, and early acceptance graduate school programs typically require high test scores that are much higher than the average test scores of Black students.

Obstacle #6: Failure to recognize the obstacles

All of these obstacles can be overcome if you recognize their existence and how they uniquely pertain to your situation. If you are confronted with any of these obstacles, you can plan your own course schedule and advocate for yourself. You can set academic goals and seek out tutoring. You can take additional math and science classes through summer school or through on-line programs. Perhaps most importantly, you control how deeply you learn. However, if you are more focused on your grade in the class than on achieving deep levels of learning, you may be an 'A' student, but lack the level of understanding that will be expected if you are pursuing a STEM career pathway. The most important academic skill for a student pursuing a career in STEM is critical thinking. Now is the time to think critically and plan purposefully.

What You Will Need to Do

Whatever the challenges or circumstances, you must take ownership of your academic trajectory by taking the following steps if you are pursuing a STEM college major:

1. Know your school district policy for advanced class placement from elementary school through high school. For example, in some school districts your grades and test scores in 3rd grade determine the level of math and science you can take in 6th grade .
2. Know which middle school classes are available for high school credit, particularly in math and science.
3. Know the middle school grades and test scores that determine the level of math and science you can take in the 9th grade.
4. Know if you will enter high school on a trajectory to take Calculus, AP Calculus, or Dual Enrollment Calculus.
5. Know the STEM classes that can be taken as electives throughout high school such as statistics and computer science.
6. Know the available dual enrollment, virtual, or online classes offered in your school district, available through your State Department of Education, or if you can earn credit for online classes taken through a community college or online school.
7. Identify tutors, books, and videos on study skills and learning strategies to assist in developing a deep understanding of math and science.

8. Join math and science clubs, qualify for math and science honor societies, participate in math and science competitions, and attend STEM summer programs throughout middle school and high school.
9. Choose either the SAT or the ACT and begin developing a deep understanding of the math and science content areas as you enter the 9th grade with a goal of earning top test scores prior to the end of 11th grade. Prepare for the 11th-grade PSAT, as it can qualify you for National Merit Scholarship consideration.
10. Develop your college and scholarship lists throughout high school as you work to prepare yourself to be a top candidate for being offered college admission into a STEM major and awarded multiple STEM scholarships.

There is another option for the most self-motivated students. Go to the CollegeBoard website and identify the most relevant AP classes pertaining to your STEM aspirations, i.e., math, science, computer science, statistics, etc. If the classes are not offered at your high school or you are otherwise unable to take the classes, look for online opportunities, or purchase the materials and teach yourself. You do not have to actually take the AP class to register for the AP exam. While this will not be an easy option, doing so will establish you as a self-motivated STEM-focused student when applying to colleges, and may very well expand your scholarship opportunities.

Even if you fall short of achieving all ten steps, each step that you are able to achieve will better prepare you to get into an HBCU and to succeed once you get there. Keep in mind that collectively, these 10 steps are intended to expand both your college and scholarship options.

Know The Facts

While the language of math is difficult to understand for many students, math is considered the most critical high school subject by many colleges and universities due to the critical-thinking and problem-solving skills taught in math and applicable to every discipline, both STEM and non-STEM. Many colleges and universities view calculus as a gateway class—one that is required for students to be considered for admission, even for non-STEM majors. Data from the National Center for Education Statistics, *"Advanced mathematics and science courses,"* notes that less than 2 in 10 (16%) high school students take calculus. The National Center for Education Statistics reports the following racial disparities in calculus course taking: (Indicator 13)

- 45% of Asian students take calculus
- 18% of White students take calculus
- 10% of Hispanic students take calculus
- 6% of Black students take calculus

Frequently, many students cannot take calculus in high school, because they did not leave middle school on an advanced math and science trajectory. Based on results from "*The National Assessment of Educational Progress for Mathematics*," only 1 in 100 Black students score at the advanced level in math by 4th grade and drop to less than 1 in 100 scoring at the advanced level in math by 12th grade.

4th Grade Math Performance (2022):

- 1% Advanced
- 14% Proficient
- 40% Basic
- 45% Below Basic

8th Grade Math Performance (2022):

- 1% Advanced
- 8% Proficient
- 29% Basic
- 62% Below Basic

12th Grade Math Performance (2019):

- <1% Advanced
- 7% Proficient
- 26% Basic
- 66% Below Basic

While the math performance level of Black students is disappointingly low, no racial group achieves greater than 50% math proficiency by 12th grade. Consequently, as all students move through school, their math proficiency is at its lowest in high school, where it matters the most—at least as it pertains to enrolling in college, pursuing a STEM career pathway, and qualifying for scholarships based on grades and test scores.

Students who do not take calculus in high school often find themselves at a disadvantage in their introduction to calculus class in college where the class moves at a fast pace and professors expect students to have a foundational understanding of calculus. The University of California's 2024 Statement on Mathematics notes:

> A student intending a STEM major (including Data Science or Computer Science) at the college level is well-advised to take Calculus or Pre-calculus, whereas others may find courses such as AP Statistics more useful.

For students pursuing a STEM career pathway, higher level math and science are stepping stones for being offered admission to college, accepted into your major, preparation for your academic curriculum in college, and then as part of the comprehensive knowledge you are expected to demonstrate on the MCAT and various licensing exams. Anderson and Burdman, in their National Association of College Admission Counseling research, *"A New Calculus for College Admissions: How Policy, Practice, and Perceptions of High School Math Education Limit Equitable Access to College,"* reports one admission officer as saying:

> *"Calculus is an easy answer to a complicated question. Institutions are looking for a simple gatekeeper. We are looking for ways to determine excellent and extraordinary students." (p. 8)*

The research also notes:

> At many highly selective colleges and universities, a preponderance of first-year students arrive on campus with calculus under their belts, a phenomenon that exists even at a small, private, liberal arts institution. Consider Wesleyan University, where 79 percent of the incoming fall 2021 class had completed math through calculus—a rate that far exceeds the most recently documented national trends. (p. 9)

The reason for helping you to understand all of the obstacles that you might be forced to overcome is to assist you in understanding the magnitude to which HBCUs have responded to these obstacles. The history of HBCUs is to educate Black students who were discriminated against or denied education. So it stands to reason, that even today, if a student has been discriminated against or denied the opportunity of taking the highest level of STEM classes during high school, HBCUs are ready, willing, and able to provide a pathway for virtually any student into a STEM career if the student is willing to work hard and commit themselves to pursuing their aspirations.

Wayna Wondwossen, in her National Science Foundation article, *"The Science Behind HBCU Success,"* notes:

> Historically Black colleges and universities have proven to be extremely effective in graduating Black students, particularly in STEM. While HBCUs enroll about 9% of Black undergraduates in the U.S., they graduate a significantly higher percentage in critical fields such as engineering, mathematics and biological sciences. HBCUs represent seven of the top eight institutions that graduate the highest number of Black undergraduate students who go on to earn S&E [Science and Engineering] doctorates.

While only enrolling 9 percent of Black undergraduate students in the U.S., HBCUs produce:

- 29.9 percent of Blacks in agriculture
- 27.8 percent of Blacks in the physical sciences
- 25.5 percent of Blacks in mathematics
- 24.7 percent of Blacks in biological sciences
- 15.7 percent of Blacks who earn science and engineering doctorates

HBCUs produce these successes by:

- Affirming the scholarship of Black people
- Creating a culture where the philosophy is to enable students to succeed, not weed them out

- Creating an institutional belief system that "it takes a village" where everyone on campus from the cafeteria to the Office of the President shares the mission and is invested in student success
- Cultivating a love of science in students who may have hated science in high school
- Cultivating a "can do" attitude in achieving mastery in math and science

HBCUs are so successful in preparing students to pursue careers in STEM that the National Science Foundation created the HBCU STEM Undergraduate Success Research Center (STEM-US), lead by researchers from Morehouse College, Spelman College, and Virginia State University to study and model the successful practices at HBCUs.

Another example of HBCU STEM success is the annual HBCU Battle of the Brains, an HBCU academic national championship as well as an experiential diversity recruiting showcase of top Black talent from colleges and universities across the country. HBCUs send their best and brightest teams to compete among the 30 teams from throughout the country. Seven teams move onto the Finals to determine the annual HBCU Battle of the Brains Champion.

Teams are typically composed of 5-8 students of which at least 50% identify as women and at least 50% identify as Black or are of the African diaspora, if institutionally applicable. A successful team will be comprised of (but not limited to) students from the following majors:

- Accounting
- Communications
- Computer Science
- Data Science/Analytics
- Digital Media
- Engineering (various)
- Finance

- Marketing
- Mathematics

Teams are encouraged to incorporate design, policy, business, and STEM components into their business solutions.

Institutional Scholarship Prizes:

- First Place Prize – $50,000
- Second Place Prize – $20,000
- Third Place Prize – $10,000

Individual Scholarship Prizes:

- Dell Technologies – $2,000
- ebay – $5,000

Winning teams represent the following HBCUs:

- 2024: Fisk University
- 2023: Alabama State University
- 2022: Fisk University
- 2020: Prairie View A&M University
- 2019: Prairie View A&M University
- 2018: Florida A&M University
- 2017: Paul Quinn College

If you are nearing the end of high school or are a community college transfer student, even if you have not taken calculus or did not meet the ACT benchmark scores in math and science, you can be comforted in knowing that if you are committed to pursuing a STEM pathway, attending an HBCU can provide the needed support to deepen your competency in math and science and propel you into a career in STEM.

HBCUs and STEM

The American Institute of Physics' report, *"The Time is Now: Systemic Changes to Increase African Americans with Bachelor's Degrees in Physics and Astronomy,"* notes how Black college students in science experience microaggressions and discrimination from non-Black peers, while peers of the same race/ethnicity/gender provide valuable social and academic support. Cultivating an environment where peers support you, and professors believe in you, are huge contributors to HBCU success in graduating Blacks in STEM majors.

The type of HBCU and scholarship opportunities presented in this book respond to other findings in the report:

- Paying for college is a primary concern for many students and their families. Access to adequate financial aid resources can be either a hindrance or a facilitator for persistence, especially for Black students and students on STEM trajectories.
- Black students frequently learn that their high school education did not prepare them for their introductory college courses and are in need of academic support, encouragement, and transitional services.
- The natural stress associated with college-level study in STEM contributes to the adverse emotional and mental health of Black students when compounded with the structural racism and sexism of some institutions.
- Students need environments that provide guidance in developing "academic capital," in such areas as relationships, information, and resources to support understanding how the academic process works, as well as strategies to be successful.
- Students need university departments that cultivate social relationships with peers for formulating study groups and sharing day-to-day departmental information.

Cherly Talley, Professor of Psychology and Neuroscience at Virginia State University, describes what she has learned from Black science students:

> I taught for 15 years at a PWI, where I brought my love of science and inquiry into the classroom. When I came to Virginia State University eight years ago, I quickly realized that my students didn't share my enthusiasm for science. In fact, they were science averse.
>
> So, I did what I was trained to do. I dove into the literature and taught myself about teaching and learning in African American populations. I soon discovered it had nothing to do with gaps or students not being smart enough or trained well enough. It was an attitudinal barrier that kept getting in the way. "I hate science," they'd say, or "they told me I'm not good at science." It was one story after another.
>
> The more I researched education, the more I saw the real issue. These students had never truly experienced science, and it's easy to hate something you don't understand. So, I went on a mission to excite them about the thing I loved.
>
> My research team and I started out working with VSU seniors, and we found that they were successful academically once their beliefs, attitude or behaviors toward STEM fields changed. I wanted to see if we could apply these same strategies to freshmen, and that became my first NSF grant. We taught upperclassmen to model the right mindset and habits for incoming freshmen and soon, we had students graduating in STEM disciplines in four to five years. Now, we're training VSU students to mentor seniors in high school. (Wondwossen, 2020)

Professor Talley's experiences at Virginia State is reflective of the overall success of HBCUs and the role that HBCUs play in ensuring that Blacks have equitable access to STEM jobs. The United Negro College Fund report, *"The Impact of HBCUs on Diversity in STEM Fields,"* notes the long standing inequitable and underrepresentation of Black students entering into STEM occupations:

> Black and White students across the country intend to pursue STEM degrees at similar rates, but Black students in any STEM field struggle to achieve comparable representation in degree attainment. The Penn Center for Minority Serving Institutions reports, for example, that Black students studying engineering earned only 4.2% of bachelor's degrees in 2012 across the United States, while white students earned 68.1%.
>
> The U.S. Department of Education reports that, among public high schools serving predominantly African American students, less than one-third of schools offer calculus and about 40% offer physics. African American students represent 16% of the country's high school students, yet only nine percent of them take an advanced placement course. It is for these reasons, among others, that many disadvantaged African American students are not prepared to pursue and succeed in a STEM degree in college.

The report goes on to note that despite these disparities in Black representation in STEM careers, HBCUs do a much better job than other schools in preparing Black students to pursue STEM degrees:

> 25 percent of African American graduates with STEM degrees come from HBCUs. HBCUs graduated 46 percent of Black women who earned degrees in STEM disciplines between 1995 and 2004. Eight HBCUs were among the top 20 institutions to award the most science and engineering bachelor's degrees to Black graduates from 2008-2012. HBCUs are the institution of origin among almost 30% of Black graduates of science and engineering doctorate programs.

If you are a teacher, counselor, parent, or student who questions whether the quality of education at HBCUs is comparable to the quality of education at non-HBCUs, consider the broad ranging agreements that HBCUs have with other schools. HBCUs have many guaranteed pathways into and through colleges and universities on the U.S. News and World Reports Best National University Rankings.

Princeton Alliance for Collaborative Research and Innovation: A research partnership between Princeton and Howard University; Jackson State University Prairie View A&M University; Spelman College; and the University of Maryland Eastern Shore. The research collaborative explores areas from science and technology to voting patterns.

Yale Alliance for Scholarship, Collaboration, Engagement, Networking, and Development: Yale will commit $2 million annually, for a total of $10 million, to this initiative. ASCEND will support research collaborations between HBCU and Yale faculty, provide resources for HBCU faculty research projects, and expand pathway programs for HBCU students. These programs, planned in collaboration with HBCU partner institutions, commit to increasing representation and amplifying the significant contributions of HBCUs in shaping the academic landscape. Partner schools are: Hampton University; Jackson State University; North Carolina A&T State University; Claflin University; Morehouse College; Morgan State University; and Tuskegee University. Faculty and students from these partner institutions are eligible to participate in ASCEND programs.

Caltech 3/2 Program which allows students from Spelman College to earn 2 degrees in 5 years—a liberal arts degree from Spelman (3 years) and a bachelor's degree from Caltech (2 years).

Similar to the Spelman-Caltech 3/2 Program, Xavier University of Louisiana offers pathways through Georgia Tech and the University of Notre-Dame, as well as a combined **BS/MD Program with Baylor College of Medicine** and an early assurance program with the University of Southern California School of Biokinesiology and Physical Therapy.

Howard University, Morehouse College, and Spelman College are part of the **Stanford-HBCU Exchange Program**, which provides a cultural and academic enrichment experience for students from member institutions.

Tougaloo College and Brown University have had an exchange agreement since 1964. Sofia Barnett's article, *"'The stars aligning': Students reflect on Tougaloo-Brown exchange semester, share advice for applicants,"* notes the value of the experience through the eyes of a Tougaloo student:

> Vivienne Diaz said that she chose to attend Tougaloo to combat the feelings of isolation she experienced after receiving a "whitewashed" education in her hometown.
>
> Diaz credited much of her ability to successfully navigate the different institutional channels at Brown to her Tougaloo advisor, Melissa McCoy, and Nirva LaFortune MA '19, former assistant director of the Curricular Resource Center for Peer Advising at Brown.
>
> "I really felt like I put down some valuable roots and made great connections," she said.
>
> Matthew McKee came to Brown from Tougaloo this summer as a research assistant for Professor of Physics and Engineering Jay Tang in search of an opportunity to "research something new, somewhere new," he said.
>
> McKee expressed feeling supported by both Brown and Tougaloo during his exchange summer, noting that he received a housing stipend from Tougaloo, as well as a $6,000 stipend from the University. He also received extensive counseling from his Tougaloo mentor, Wendy White of the Jackson Heart Study Undergraduate Training and Education Center.

Morehouse College and Spelman College are listed among the 2023-24 top producers of Fulbright Scholars. In 2023, 19 HBCUs were recognized by the U.S. Department of State as Fulbright HBCU Institutional Leaders. Among the 19 schools are Howard University, Fayetteville State University, Jackson State University, Morgan State University, Tuskegee University, and Virginia State University.

Anyone willing to look beyond negative stereotypes and misinformation will find that HBCUs offer many more opportunities than most would imagine. However, beyond band performances, step shows, and homecoming celebrations, discovering academic and employment pathways will require engaging in research and exploring the many options and opportunities.

Which HBCU is Right for You?

Take a holistic approach to your college research. Beyond the normal considerations of costs, campus, and community, expand your research to include relationships each school has established with other schools and employers. These relationships will include dual degree and exchange programs, internship and mentorship programs, scholarships, and companies that are the top employers of graduates.

The Career Communications Group's report, *"2024 Top Supporters of HBCU Engineering Schools,"* identifies the top industry supporters and top government and nonprofit employers of HBCU engineering schools.

Top HBCU Industry Supporters

1. Lockheed Martin
2. IBM
3. Microsoft
4. Apple
5. The Boeing Company
6. Leidos
7. Northrop Grumman
8. RTX
9. Amazon
10. Abbott
11. Google
12. General Dynamics Information Technology
13. General Motors
14. Intel
15. Micron

Top HBCU Government and Nonprofit Supporters

1. National Science Foundation (NSF)
2. NASA
3. Advancing Minorities' Interest in Engineering
4. National Security Agency
5. U.S. Department of Energy (DoE)
6. U.S. Army Corps of Engineers (USACE)
7. U.S. Department of Defense (DoD)
8. U.S. Department of Education
9. U.S. Department of Transportation (DoT)
10. Sandia Research Laboratory

Given the wide range of potential STEM pathways, it is advisable to allow "What if" questions to guide your college research.

"What if I change my mind about pursuing a career as a biochemist or biophysicist?" If you are passionate about biology or physics, then you would still be able to pursue a career as a biological technician.

"What if I change my mind about pursuing a career as a nuclear engineer?" If you are passionate about nuclear research, then a nuclear technician still earns a median salary of $101,740 per year.

"What if I change my mind about pursuing a career as a computer programmer?" If you are passionate about computers, then you pursue a career as a computer technician or a computer support specialist.

Considering majors beyond your first choice major is not only good strategy, but supported by data from the National Center for Education Statistics study, *"Beginning College Students Who Change Their Majors Within 3 Years of Enrollment,"* regarding how frequently students change majors:

- 52 percent of students whose original declared major was mathematics switched majors within 3 years. Students majoring in mathematics changed majors at a rate higher than that of students in all other fields, both STEM and non-STEM, except the natural sciences.

- 40 percent of students whose original declared major was natural sciences switched majors within 3 years.
- 32 percent of students whose original declared major was engineering and engineering technology switched majors within 3 years.
- 28 percent of students whose original declared major was in computer and information sciences switched majors within 3 years.

For many students, college is the first time they have the opportunity to engage in learning what is actually required for pursuing a particular career pathway, including what they are expected to know, what they are expected to do, and the type of environment they will be working in over the course of a good part of their adult life. The exploratory process, for some students, reinforces deeply and long-held passionate areas of learning. During high school, Kimberly was not only clear in her passion for studying math and science, she was clear in her math calculation when applying to college:

Full Scholarship = $0 Student/Parent PLUS Loan Debt

Upon graduating from high school, Kimberly was profiled in the article, *"Student Overcomes the Odds to Receive $1.8 Million In Scholarships, Including Full Scholarships to 6 Top Colleges."* One of schools offering a full scholarship was a top liberal arts college where she could explore her passions in math and chemistry for 2 years before declaring a major. During this exploratory period, she was reaffirmed in her passions and went on to receive a BA in Math and Chemistry. Her stellar undergraduate academic record, together with the leadership and service reflected on her CV, was rewarded with 6 full graduate school scholarships. In addition to her 6 graduate school scholarships, she received a *NSF Graduate Research Fellowship* (GRFP) and is now about to receive her PhD in Math. She will leave college as a 26-year-old Dr. Kimberly Hadaway. Through her time in college and in graduate school, she has yet to affirm a specific career pathway, but has learned that a woman of color holding a PhD in math has many options from teaching K-12 or college math to working for NASA, DoD, IBM, or the CIA—the opportunities are endless.

If, on the other hand, she had not discovered her passion in math or chemistry, the choice of majors at her college relating to her passions in math and science ranged from bioinformatics, genomics & proteomics to geosciences. Having the option of changing majors within your school would allow you to keep your scholarship, while pursuing other areas of learning and other career pathways.

Many high school students are misinformed in believing that a pathway into a STEM career must lead through a research university and that liberal arts colleges are only focused on the arts and humanities. Not only are students misinformed, but there are many HBCU liberal arts colleges with a long history of success in preparing Black students for careers in STEM, such as:

- **Bennett College,** a partner school in the VA-NC Alliance for Minority Participation in STEM.
- **Claflin University,** which received a $5 million STEM grant from Google.
- **Dillard University,** which received a $1.25 million grant for STEM Education and Research.
- **Johnson C. Smith University,** which received a $1 million U.S. Department of Homeland Security Grant.
- **Kentucky State University,** which received a $7 million grant from the National Science Foundation to expand agriculture technology (AgTech).
- **Lane College,** which received a $815,000 grant from the National Science Foundation to increase the number of students entering graduate and professional school in STEM fields.
- **Morehouse College,** $2 million investment by Google to support talent development and innovation in STEM.
- **Rust College,** which partnered with the University of Mississippi for a dual degree program in engineering.

- **Spelman College,** $200,000 investment by Deloitte Foundation to support students pursuing STEM fields.
- **Xavier University of Louisiana,** known as the nation's top producer of Black graduates who go on to become doctors, and its distinctions don't end there; according to NSF, Xavier is ranked third in the nation for undergraduate sources of African American students who go on to complete doctoral degrees in the physical and Earth sciences and is ranked fifth for those who go on to complete doctoral degrees in the life sciences. Furthermore, despite Xavier's neuroscience program launching just a few years ago (2017), the National Center for Educational Statistics (NCES) Integrated Postsecondary Education Data System (IPEDS) found that Xavier ranks highly in the number of African American 2022 baccalaureate degree neuroscience graduates.

Whether the right fit for you is in a liberal arts college like those mentioned here or a research university like North Carolina A&T State University, Florida A&M University, or Alabama State University, you have many choices among HBCUs to explore STEM disciplines and pursue a STEM career.

Program Accreditation

As you research colleges and programs, there are certifying organizations you may use to learn more about the accreditation of the program.

ABET: The world's leading accreditation body for programs in applied and natural science, computing, engineering and engineering technology. ABET's scope has grown beyond its original engineering and technology focus. ABET has 4 accreditation commissions:

- Applied and Natural Sciences Accreditation Commission
- Computing Accreditation Commission
- Engineering Accreditation Commission
- Engineering Technology Accreditation Commission

Aviation Accreditation Board International: To achieve accreditation, aviation programs must satisfy the expectations of a wide range of quality criteria relating to strategic management of resources, interactions of faculty and students in the educational process and achievement of degree learning goals.

Council for Higher Education Accreditation: The CHEA Database of Accredited Institutions and Programs and other informational items are on the CHEA.org website and available to the public.

STEM Learning Academic Accreditation Council: STEM Learning Academic Accreditation Council (SLAAC) represents an innovative initiative committed to advancing education in the fields of Science, Technology, Engineering, and Mathematics.

American Council on Higher Education: A major coordinating body for more than 1,600 colleges and universities, related associations, and other organizations in the United States and abroad. ACE is the only major higher education association to represent all types of U.S. accredited, degree-granting colleges and universities.

Race and Ethnicity in Higher Education: The 2024 report follows Race and Ethnicity in Higher Education: A Status Report, released in February 2019, and Race and Ethnicity in Higher Education: 2020 Supplement, released in November 2020.

Carnegie Classification®: When pursuing a STEM major, you should consider the research classification of a school and what that means. Carnegie Classification® is the leading framework for recognizing and describing institutional diversity in U.S. higher education. In 1970, the Carnegie Commission on Higher Education began developing a classification of colleges and universities to support its program of research and policy analysis. The framework was first published in 1973 and is now updated every 3 years to reflect changes among colleges and universities.

The classification levels most pertinent to STEM is the research classification as it determines the ability of an institution to apply for federal research grants, which are worth millions of dollars in financial resources received by the college to conduct research.

HBCUs: You can research the Carnegie Classification for all 101 currently accredited HBCUs, including student enrollment, location, public or private, and undergraduate focus.

Research Classifications

R1: Doctoral Universities: Very high research activity: On average in a single year, these institutions spend at least $50 million on research & development and produce at least 70 research doctorates.

R2: Doctoral Universities: High research activity: On average in a single year, these institutions spend at least $5 million on research & development and produce at least 20 research doctorates.

D/PU: Doctoral/Professional Universities: On average in a single year, these institutions spend at least $2.5 million on research & development. Institutions that are in the R1 or R2 categories are not included.

Currently 11 of the 101 U.S. colleges and universities with R2 classification are HBCUs:

1. Clark Atlanta University
2. Florida A&M University
3. Howard University
4. Jackson State University
5. Morgan State University
6. North Carolina A&T State University
7. Prairie View A&M University
8. Southern University and A&M College
9. Tennessee State University
10. Texas Southern University
11. University of Maryland Eastern Shore

In 2024, no HBCUs have R1 classification. Jaret Riddick in his Center for Security and Emerging Technology article, *"Good News in Progress Toward Top-Tier Research Status for HBCUs?"* projects that 2 HBCUs, Howard University and North Carolina A&T State University, appear to be on track to achieve the R1 research classification.

Sarah Weissman in her Inside Higher Education article, *"Striving for the 'Gold Standard'"* quotes two HBCU leaders who talk about the importance of the R1 classification on their schools' undergraduate programs:

> Dr. Wayne A.I. Frederick, president of Howard University, notes "The types of faculty we would be able to draw would increase the type of instruction and exposure undergraduate students, in particular, would have to high-level research and faculty that are cutting-edge," he said. "It will also improve our ability to enhance innovative programming, all of which would bode well for the student body that is here."
>
> Eric Muth, a vice chancellor at North Carolina A&T State University, notes "When we want to diversify the future of the scientific community, and ensure that it stays diverse, we need to expose our undergrads to science as they're getting educated," he said. "And we need to expose them to the best and brightest science going on."

HBCUs that are approaching R1 status have had to overcome obstacles of racial bias (Source: Race, Ethnicity, and NIH Research Awards) at agencies distributing grants, misappropriation of funds (Source: Secretaries of Education, Agriculture Call on Governors to Equitably Fund Land-Grant HBCUs) by state legislatures, and other financial limitations (Source: Achieving Financial Equity and Justice for HBCUs).

STEM Dominant Graduate Programs: 3 HBCUs are among the 83 institutions classified as having STEM dominate graduate programs:

- North Carolina A&T State University
- Tuskegee University
- University Maryland Eastern Shore

These are some of the many available resources that go deeper into your college research beyond popularity and notoriety. The classification of colleges and universities impact the number and type of employers who recruit at the college, access to research funding, and the availability of research opportunities on campus and through professors.

Choosing Pathways - Ability versus Passion

First: Choose the best undergraduate pathway

In general, many STEM disciplines are vague concepts until you have an opportunity to experience first-hand food science, computer programming, quantum physics, or actuarial science. To gain such experiences will require that you actively explore classes offered in your school and community, summer programs, and visiting colleges. You might also gain experiences through clubs and community-based organizations.

It is important to explore all available options pertaining to the many STEM pathways. Talking to scientists, video game designers, engineers, and mathematicians; visiting manufacturing facilities, research facilities, and robotics labs; talking to college professors and college students; and experiencing internships and research opportunities during high school are all important to expanding your understanding of what people do in different types of jobs.

While it is important to research the salaries of particular careers, it is more important to determine if the type of job and working conditions are reflective of your interests and personality. Some jobs require working in isolation while others require working on a team with lots of other people. Which one is best for you? Some jobs require interacting with people, while other jobs require interacting with data. Which one is best for you? Some jobs require sitting behind a desk, while other jobs require traveling or being outdoors. Which one is best for you?

Second: Prepare for the Opportunities

Pursuing a STEM pathway through an HBCU will involve more than taking and performing well in math and science classes. In 2024, the Biden-Harris Administration allocated over $16 Billion in support for Historically Black Colleges and Universities (HBCUs). The historic funding allowed HBCUs to expand facilities, infrastructure, research, and summer programs. There is perhaps no greater advantage than to attend summer STEM programs offered by HBCUs for high school and middle school students. Two areas of funding, include:

> Over $1.6 billion to HBCUs through Federal grants, cooperative agreements, and other competitive funding opportunities that drive the advancement of academic and training programs, community-based initiatives, and research innovation across national priorities such as medicine and public health, climate science, agriculture, emerging technologies, and defense.
>
> Nearly $719 million in grant funding to expand STEM academic capacity and educational programs; and in other high-wage, high-demand fields such as computer science, nursing, and allied health.

Morehouse College offers elementary, middle, high school, and pre-college programs.

Spelman College offers the College Prep Institute, Early College Program, WiSTEM Program, Pre-Freshman Experience Summer Data Science Program, and Pre-Health Summer Program.

Tuskegee University offers the Afri-TREK/Sci-TREK/AgDiscovery Program, CISC Summer Experience, EXERT Summer Camp, Forestry & Natural Resources Program, STEM Summer Academy, and Architecture & Construction Science.

Xavier University of Louisiana has offered summer programs for nearly 50 years in academic enrichment, mentorship, and career exploration. They host six different opportunities for middle school and high school students to experience a rigorous academic setting in a historic black college environment for three intensive weeks!

USBE Information Technology's *"Explore STEM Camps and Programs at HBCUs"* provides an overview of programs at Tuskegee University, Howard University, and Alabama A&M University.

HBCUBuzz's *"6 HBCUs Offering Summer Programs"* provides an overview of programs at Morehouse College, Spelman College, Prairie View A&M University, Hampton University, Fisk University, and North Carolina A&T State University. You can contact schools or perform an internet search on the phrase, "name of school + summer stem programs" and "best hbcu summer stem programs."

Research HBCU Grants: Performing an internet search on the phrases "south carolina hbcu grants" or "hbcu grants" will allow you to identify grants provided by the federal government to HBCUs to support research, innovation, and degree programs. One such grant is the "NNSA (National Nuclear Security Administration) Awards HBCU Grants," which included grants to Allen University, Benedict College, Claflin University, South Carolina State University, and Voorhees University. Performing a search on the phrase "north carolina hbcu grants" allows you to identify grants such as the "Dept. of Justice Awards HBCU Consortium Grant: NC A&T Lead Institution."

Following are the titles of videos available at the writing of this book on YouTube, where you can learn more about the experiences of students participating in these programs:

- **FAA HBCU Initiative Overview:** Video of the FAA HBCU partnership.
- **HBCU Pride at the FAA:** Video of HBCU pathways into the FAA.
- **HBCU Initiative Group — Employee Spotlight:** Alan Kiel: Perspective of Texas Southern University graduate employed at the FAA.
- **HBCU Initiative Group — Employee Spotlight:** Marcus Ward: Perspective of Tuskegee University graduate employed at the FAA.
- **Texas Southern University Offers Aviation Program To Bring Diversity to Field:** Video of Texas Southern University aviation flight programs.
- **Southwest Airlines Partners With Texas HBCU To Recruit Future Black Pilots:** Video profiling Southwest Airlines

partnership with Texas HBCUs.

- **Howard Grad Makes U.S. Air Force Thunderbird History:** Video of Howard University graduate and U.S. Air Force officer who made history as part of the U.S. Air Force Thunderbirds.
- **United – Hampton University Pilots Inspiring Future aviators To Soar:** Video profiling United Airlines partnership with Hampton University.
- **Intel Invests $4.5 Million Into HBCU STEM Programs at Six Universities:** Video profiling Intel's HBCU STEM investment.
- **Jackson State Joins Google's HBCU Career Readiness Program:** Video profiling the Jackson State University Growth with Google partnership.
- **Cognosante HBCU Partner Alliance:** Video profiling the tech company, Cognosante, and its HBCU partnership.
- **Fostering Strategic Partnerships With HBCUs and HSIs:** Video profiling Oak Ridge Laboratory's support of HBCU pathways to a PhD.
- **Strada Education Foundation Strengthens Partnership With SUNO to Nurture Future Leaders:** Profiles the Strada Scholars Program at Southern University of New Orleans.
- **DoD HBCU/MI Internship:** Video Profiling the Department of Defense's HBCU internship opportunities.
- **BGE Celebrates Partnerships with Local HBCUs:** Video Profiling Baltimore Gas and Electric Company HBCU scholarship and internship opportunities.
- **IBM Partnering With HBCUs:** Video profiling the IBM HBCU Quantum Center.
- **Examining the Impact of the IBM-HBCU Quantum Center:** Video profiling IBM Quantum Center HBCU partnerships.
- **Spelman College Receives $100 Million Donation, Largest in HBCU History:** Video profiling the announcement of Spelman Colleges' $100 million donation

from a private donor.

- **HBCU Clean Energy Education Prize — Dillard University:** Video profiling the expansion of the Dillard University clean energy curriculum as a result of being awarded the multi-million dollar prize.
- **HBCU Clean Energy Education Prize — Tennessee State University:** Video profiling the expansion of the Tennessee State University clean energy curriculum as a result of being awarded the multi-million dollar prize.

Third: Develop your network and plan for scholarships

Every opportunity in which you become involved is an opportunity to build a relationship, receive a recommendation letter, or make a connection to a program or scholarship opportunity. Planning for scholarships requires developing a scholarship table, which will continually evolve as you identify scholarships and application periods which may be far into the future. While high school seniors or community college students may identify scholarships for which they can apply for immediately, other scholarships may only be available to first-, second-, or third-year college students. Consequently, these will become scholarships for which students "plan" to apply in the future and scholarships for which students have years to make themselves competitive applicants.

Finally: Increase your financial literacy

Invest in your own future by knowing how to research costs (not only tuition, room, and board, but books, application fees, exam fees, personal expenses, transportation expenses, and the cost of health insurance), calculate the interest you will pay on student loans, and how much interest will accumulate over the course of college, graduate school, and medical school. Accept the responsibility of understanding which scholarships are one-time awards versus those that are renewable, as well as understanding the academic standing required to renew scholarships. While the HBCU experience will be filled with homecoming celebrations, parties, and pledging a fraternity or sorority, do not allow such experiences to distract you from your purpose for attending college or keeping the scholarships needed to pay for college.

STEM is a broad discipline covering a multitude of careers in each area (i.e., Science, Technology, Engineering, and Mathematics). Consequently, I have chosen to focus each of the following chapters on careers related to the projected 2023-33 fasting growing occupations. I have chosen to supplement these occupations with areas that are currently being funded at HBCUs. Through this combination, you should have a range of careers and college majors to consider.

Unless you have had extensive experiences working in STEM, like solving mathematical or statistical models, robotics, video game design, or had medical research experiences, you should approach STEM careers broadly. This means that if you really like biology, then explore a wide range of careers pertaining to the biological sciences. If you like robotics, then explore a wide range of careers in robotics and mechatronics. Proceeding in such a manner will provide insight and experiences across different career pathways, but pathways that have a core connection—your passion.

HBCU Science Pathways

HBCUs are expanding opportunities to increase Black representation across multiple areas of science from developing computer chips to environmental justice. On February 9, 2024, the *"Biden-Harris Administration Announces Over $5 Billion from the CHIPS and Science Act for Research, Development, and Workforce,"* led to the development of the HBCU Chips Network:

> The HBCU CHIPS Network will engage the HBCU community in a comprehensive plan to support the manufacture of microelectronic products with the benefit that this strategy will effectively reach underserved communities across the national landscape. This effort will further provide an opportunity to design and implement innovative approaches that optimize resources across diverse institutions – and with lasting impacts for traditionally untapped citizens and communities.

23 HBCUs are part of the initial partnership with additional HBCUs planning to participate in the grant. Participating institutions will be responsible for the science and engineering required in every facet of microchip development.

On August 7, 2024, Dillard University was one of the recipients of a $19.94 million community change grant from the U.S. Environmental Protection Agency (EPA).

> This grant, totaling $19.94 million, will allow Dillard University to create community resilience hubs, expand bike sharing and electric vehicle charger access, retrofit buildings to reduce greenhouse gas emissions, launch non-degree training programs in clean energy and climate resilience, and enhance community resilience in Orleans, St. Tammany, and Washington Parishes.

Through this federal award, the project will provide up to 300 families with e-bikes, expand bike-sharing programs, install EV chargers, and retrofit public buildings with energy-efficient systems. Dillard University will also spearhead new educational programs in clean energy and climate resilience.

If you have a love for science, there are many pathways that take less time, cost less money, and still earn comparable salaries as medical documents, and higher salaries than registered nurses. While there is nothing wrong with pursuing a career in medicine or nursing, you should ask yourself the question, "Do I aspire to become a doctor or nurse, because those are careers with which I am most familiar?" Another question is, "What careers do you associate with science?"

Enviva, a global renewable energy company specializing in sustainable wood bioenergy, has created a pipeline for HBCU STEM students through a multi-year recruiting and career development pipeline with North Carolina A&T University, North Carolina Central University, Alabama A&M University, and Jackson State University.

Bethune-Cookman University: NASA MUREP DEAP Institute of Environmental Intelligence for Advanced Space-based Earth Sciences. The project will establish a DEAP Institute focusing on machine learning-based development of a virtual constellation of satellites that will capture changing water levels, from events such as storm flooding to multi-decadal time scales, such as sea level rise. NASA tracks sea level changes and its causes from space.

Morgan State University: Long-Term, High-Resolution Urban Aerosol Database for Research, Education and Outreach. Through innovative data analysis algorithms, including ML/AI methods, this project will produce a high-resolution, open-access, and user-friendly urban aerosol database focusing on the Baltimore-Washington area. The database will also be used in both classroom teaching and scientific outreach, accompanied by online tools and educational materials bringing new, authentic Earth science education to local schools and communities.

North Carolina A&T State University: DEAP Institute: Harnessing Data Science for Flood Monitoring and Management. Three North Carolina-based HBCUs will work together on this project developed to harness data science for flood monitoring and management.

North Carolina Central University: Capacity Building to Support the Machine Learning-Based Detection of Floods and other Natural Hazard Impacts in the Department of Environmental, Earth and Geospatial Sciences at North Carolina Central University. This project will create training, data resources, and opportunities to use machine learning/artificial intelligence to identify and measure the impact of flood events and other natural hazards such as earthquakes, hurricanes, drought, wildfires, and more.

Prairie View A&M University: Department of Transportation first-ever HBCU to lead a University Transportation Center. Other schools to receive a portion of a $435 million grant for development of interoperable technology systems include: Benedict College; Central State University; Florida A&M University; Howard University; Jackson State University; Morgan State University; Morehouse College; North Carolina A&T State University; South Carolina State University; Tennessee State University; and Texas Southern University.

Howard University: University Affiliated Research Center (UARC). The research center is sponsored by the U.S. Air Force and focused on tactical autonomy. It is the first university-affiliated research center associated with an HBCU and the first sponsored by the Air Force. Other participating schools are: Bowie State University; Florida Memorial University; Hampton University; Jackson State University; Norfolk State University; Tougaloo College; and Tuskegee University.

Department of Commerce Connecting-Minority-Communities Program: Provides funding for 43 HBCUs to purchase broadband internet, equipment, and IT personnel.

Department of Energy Accelerated, Inclusive Research (FAIR) Program: Provides over $35 million to build research capacity, infrastructure, and expertise for Florida A&M University; Howard

University; Morgan State University; Prairie View A&M University; and West Virginia State University.

BP HBCU Fellowship Program: As part of BP's HBCU Fellowship Program, 3 HBCUs received $1.35 million each, covering five full scholarships per year at each school for three years – a total of 45 full scholarships. Students who successfully complete the program are provided with opportunities for additional development, including internships:

- Florida A&M University
- North Carolina A&T University
- Prairie View A&M University

BRPH Future Achievers Scholarship: Architecture or engineering majors at:

- Tuskegee University
- Florida A&M University

CodeHouse Scholars Initiative: The CodeHouse Scholars Initiative (CHSI) mentors, prepares and invests in Black, Latinx, and Native American students, in their first year of college, for a career in the tech industry. As a scholar, students will be able to receive up to $20,000 academic scholarships for a tech-related degree. Must be enrolled for the first time at one of the five (5) participating HBCUs:

- Clark Atlanta University
- Howard University
- Morehouse College
- North Carolina A&T State University
- Spelman College

Not only do the careers in the following table reflect the passionate and purposeful study of science, they represent many different applications of science from the study of food, to the study of human bones, to the study of planets and stars, to the study of people and civilizations. The following table reflects information collected from the U.S. Bureau of Labor Statistics Occupational Outlook Handbook: *"Life, Physical, and Social Science Occupations"* for the array of science related careers.

Career	Salary	Description
Agricultural and Food Scientists	$76,400	Agricultural and food scientists research ways to improve the efficiency and safety of agricultural establishments and products.
Anthropologists and Archaeologists	$63,800	Anthropologists and archaeologists study the origin, development, and behavior of humans.
Atmospheric Scientists, Including Meteorologists	$92,860	Atmospheric scientists study, report on, and forecast the weather and climate.
Biochemists and Biophysicists	$107,460	Biochemists and biophysicists study the chemical and physical principles of living things and of biological processes.
Chemists and Materials Scientists	$87,180	Chemists and materials scientists research and analyze the chemical properties of substances to develop new materials, products, or knowledge.
Conservation Scientists and Foresters	$68,300	Conservation scientists and foresters manage the land quality of forests, parks, rangelands, and other natural resources.
Economists	$115,730	Economists conduct research, prepare reports, and evaluate issues related to monetary and fiscal policy. They also may collect and analyze statistical data.
Environmental Scientists and Specialists	$78,980	Environmental scientists and specialists use their knowledge of the natural sciences to protect the environment and human health.
Epidemiologists	$81,390	Epidemiologists are public health workers who investigate patterns and causes of disease and injury.

Career	Salary	Description
Geographers	$90,880	Geographers study the Earth and the distribution of its land, features, and inhabitants.
Geoscientists	$92,580	Geoscientists study the physical aspects of the Earth.
Historians	$72,890	Historians research, analyze, interpret, and write about the past by studying historical documents and sources.
Hydrologists	$88,770	Hydrologists study how water moves across and through the Earth's crust.
Microbiologists	$85,470	Microbiologists study microorganisms such as bacteria, algae, and fungi.
Physicists and Astronomers	$149,530	Physicists and astronomers study the interactions of matter and energy.
Political Scientists	$132,350	Political scientists study the origin, development, and operation of political systems.
Psychologists	$92,740	Psychologists study cognitive, emotional, and social processes and behavior by observing, interpreting, and recording how people relate to one another and to their environments.
Sociologists	$101,770	Sociologists study society and social behavior.
Urban and Regional Planners	$81,800	Urban and regional planners develop comprehensive plans and programs for use of land and physical facilities in cities, counties, metropolitan areas, and other jurisdictions.
Zoologists and Wildlife Biologists	$70,600	Zoologists and wildlife biologists study animals, those both in captivity and in the wild, and how they interact with their ecosystems.

Begin your college research for the best HBCUs for science by performing an internet search on the phrase, "best HBCUs for science." The search is likely to result in more results for STEM in general, so you can change the phrase to "best HBCUs for + career or major, " e.g., best HBCUs for zoologists or best HBCUs for animal science. While the first results will be "*Best Zoology Degree Colleges in the U.S.*" or "*Colleges Offering a Wildlife Science Major*," you might find your way to zoology through animal science and a link at HBCULifeStyle, "*HBCU Colleges with Veterinary Programs: A Comprehensive Guide*," which lists the following schools:

- Tuskegee University Animal & Veterinary Sciences Degree Program
- Florida A&M University College of Agriculture and Food Sciences
- North Carolina A&T State University College of Agriculture and Environmental Sciences
- Delaware State University Department of Agriculture & Natural Resources
- Fort Valley State University Department of Veterinary Science and Public Health

Repeat this process for each area of science for which you have a passion and explore the many available career pathways.

Scholarships and Partnerships

Beginning your scholarship search for scholarships related to your desired college major or career aspirations, and that are offered by or for HBCUS, are not only directly connected to your aspirations, but are likely to have fewer applicants than national scholarship programs open to all students.

Begin your research into HBCU-specific scholarships for science by performing an internet search on the phrase, "hbcu science scholarships," "scholarships for black science majors," and "hbcu scholarships for science majors." Expand your research to using phrases including a specific major, e.g., "hbcu scholarships for chemistry majors" or "scholarships for black students majoring in chemistry."

Following are some of the scholarships pertaining to science majors and careers, some of which are only available at specific HBCUs.

American Association of Blacks in Energy (AABE) Scholarship: To provide direct input into the deliberations and developments of energy policies, regulations, emerging technologies, and environmental issues. Awards twelve scholarships at $3K each and one scholarship at $5K.

BP HBCU Fellowship Program: As part of BP's HBCU Fellowship Program, 3 HBCUs received $1.35 million each, covering five full scholarships per year at each school for three years—a total of 45 full scholarships. Students who successfully complete the program are provided with opportunities for additional development, including internships:

- Florida A&M University
- North Carolina A&T University
- Prairie View A&M University

Brown and Caldwell Minority Scholarship: Offers a $5,000 Minority Scholarship to support students who identify as minorities and are interested in pursuing a career in the environmental profession.

Department of Energy: Accelerated, Inclusive Research (FAIR) Program providing over $35 million to build research capacity, infrastructure, and expertise at institutions historically excluded from federal research and development which include:

- Florida A&M University
- Howard University
- Morgan State University
- Prairie View A&M University
- West Virginia State University

Department of Transportation: Prairie View A&M University in Texas is the first-ever HBCU to lead a University Transportation Center. Other schools to receive a portion of a $435 million grant for development of interoperable technology systems include:

- Benedict College
- Central State University
- Florida A&M University
- Howard University
- Jackson State University
- Morgan State University
- Morehouse College
- North Carolina A&T State University
- South Carolina State University
- Tennessee State University
- Texas Southern University

Development Fund for Black Students in Science and Technology: Available to black students studying STEM and enrolling at one of the following HBCUs:

Bennett College	Morehouse College
Clark Atlanta University	Morgan State University
Elizabeth City State University	North Carolina A&T State University
Fisk University	Prairie View A&M University
Florida A&M University	Southern University
Fort Valley State College	Spelman College
Hampton University	Tennessee State University
Howard University	Tuskegee University
Langston University	Wilberforce University
Lincoln University (PA)	Xavier University of Louisiana

Grow with Google: Partners with HBCU career services centers across the United States to help Black college students develop the digital skills they need to find and secure internships and jobs that will help them build successful careers. To support the program, Google has committed more than $1 million to HBCU career service centers nationwide to be distributed by TMCF.

Howard University Karsh STEM Scholars Program: The Karsh STEM Scholars Program is Howard University's premier scholarship program for high-achieving students of science, technology, engineering and mathematics disciplines, offering full scholarships for undergraduate studies and support for successful matriculation through graduate and professional studies. The Karsh STEM Scholars Program is committed to increasing the number of underrepresented minorities who earn a PhD, or combined MD/PhD in STEM-related disciplines.

Stantec Equity & Diversity Scholarship: Along with the scholarship, students received seven paid internships within Stantec Transportation, Buildings, Environmental Services, and Water teams in North America. Selected students are passionate about their studies and future careers which are in a wide range of disciplines including computer programming, Indigenous studies, psychology, engineering, neuroscience, economics, mechatronics, biology, animal sciences, and more.

UNCF Chevron Corporate Scholars Program: The UNCF Chevron Corporate Scholars Program will award a two-year, renewable scholarship for up to $15,000 (up to $7,500 freshmen year, up to $7,500 sophomore year) to highly capable future leaders who demonstrate academic achievement, strong leadership skills and an interest in the energy industry. Must be a graduating high school senior planning to enroll as a full-time, first-year student at an HBCU.

USDA/1890 National Scholars Program: Available to high school seniors entering their freshman year of college and rising college sophomores and juniors. The USDA/1890 National Scholars Program will provide full tuition, employment, employee benefits, fees, books, and room and board each year for up to 4 years to selected students pursuing a bachelor's degree at the following universities:

- Alabama A&M University
- Alcorn State University
- Central State University
- Delaware State University
- Florida A&M University
- Fort Valley State University

- Kentucky State University
- Langston University
- Lincoln University (MO)
- North Carolina A&T State University
- Prairie View A&M University
- South Carolina State University
- Southern University and A&M College
- Tennessee State University
- Tuskegee University
- University of Arkansas Pine Bluff
- University of Maryland Eastern Shore
- Virginia State University
- West Virginia State University

HBCU-specific scholarships are extensively covered in the *HBCU Scholarships and more...**. However, to jump start your scholarship research, begin by performing internet searches on phrases containing:

- Race
- Gender
- Field of Study
- Level of Study (i.e., undergraduate, graduate, doctorate, etc.)

Following are examples of using these phrases:

- "undergraduate scholarships for black students in stem"
- "graduate fellowships for mechanical engineering"
- "graduate fellowships for women in stem"
- "graduate fellowships for black students"

Performing an internet search in this way will show pages and pages of scholarships from across the internet. However, to focus your search on UNCF (United Negro College Fund) and TMCF (Thurgood

Marshall College Fund) scholarships, use search phrases like the following:

- Example, "site: uncf.org stem scholarships" **[site: + uncf. org + stem scholarships]** limits the search to UNCF-affiliated scholarships or scholarships posted on the UNCF website. Continue to change the "stem" part of the phrase to other terms, e.g., women, black male, minority, computer engineering, cybersecurity, etc.
- Example, "site: tmcf.org stem scholarships" **[site: + tmcf. org + stem scholarships]** limits the search to TMCF-affiliated scholarships or scholarships posted on the TMCF website. Continue to change the "stem" part of the phrase to other terms, e.g., women, black male, minority, computer engineering, cybersecurity, etc.

Resources

Associations and networking organizations for science:

- American Academy of Arts and Sciences
- American Association for the Advancement of Science
- American Association of Black Physician Scientists
- American Association of Blacks in Energy
- American Association of University Women
- American Ceramic Society
- Association for Women in Science
- Benjamin Banneker Association
- Black & Brown Founders
- Black Founders
- Black in Marine Science
- Black Microbiologists Association
- Black Professionals in STEM
- Black Science Network
- Black Women in Ecology, Evolution, and Marine Science
- Black Women in Science & Engineering
- Conference for African American Researchers in the Mathematical Sciences
- Earth Science Women's Network
- Enhancing Diversity in Graduate Education

- Geoprofessional Business Association
- Harvard Society of Black Scientists and Engineers
- Hidden Genius Project
- Institute for Operations Research and the Management Sciences
- Materials Research Society
- National Academies of Sciences Engineering and Medicine
- National Academy of Medicine
- National Academy of Sciences
- National Alliance for Inclusive & Diverse STEM Faculty
- National Association of Black Geoscientists
- National Association of Black STEM Teachers
- National Girls Collaborative Project
- National Institutes of Health Women in Biomedical Careers
- National Science Foundation
- National Society of Black Physicists
- Opportunity Hub
- ProActive Network
- Scientific Societies
- Society for Science
- Science
- Science Advances
- Science Immunology
- Science News
- Science Robotics
- Science Signaling
- Science Translational Medicine
- Scientific American
- Scientista
- Society of Black Archaeologists
- Tapia Center for Excellence and Equity in Education
- The Algebra Project
- The Knowledge House
- We Build Black
- Young People's Project

HBCU Technology Pathways

If you have a love for gaming, have enjoyed a computer science class, or have participated in a coding camp, technology pathways through HBCUs provide not only opportunities to study what you enjoy, but provide direct pathways into some of America's largest tech companies.

As reflected in all STEM-related careers, Blacks use technology, but are underrepresented in technology careers. Through my personal experience working with high school students, I have experienced first-hand large numbers of Black high school students who spend hours playing video games, while devoting a small fraction of the available time to their math and science studies. This dynamic leads to predictable outcomes. Amanda Lenhart in *"Chapter 3: Video Games Are Key Elements in Friendships for Many Boys,"* found that 83% of Black teens play video games. The International Game Developers Association report, *"Diversity in the Game Industry"* shows despite 83% of Black teens playing video games, Black game developers only make up 5% of the gaming industry.

HBCUs are trying to increase the representation of Blacks in this sector of the tech industry by connecting the passion of Black students to play games with the academic training to develop games. Some of these initiatives and opportunities include:

HBCU Game Jam: In 2024, HBCU Game Jam, developed by the Spelman College Innovation Lab, is exclusively for HBCU students, bringing together students from all over the United States allowing students to connect with their HBCU peers. The HBCU Game Jam is an opportunity for beginner students to learn the interdisciplinary process of game creation: the creative and the technical. Students are introduced to the concept of "Hackathon," which is an event where participants engage in rapid and collaborative engineering over a relatively short period of time (24 or 48 hours). The HBCU

Game Jam lasts for 24 hours.

Johnson C. Smith University: In 2020, became the first HBCU to offer an Esports Lab, Esports Club, and Esports and Gaming Management academic program. However, there are other North Carolina HBCUs providing gaming programs and competitions. Benedict College in South Carolina is the first HBCU to offer an Esports degree and offer a gaming room.

HBCU Esports League: Is the largest culture and lifestyle program on Twitch, has intense gaming competitions with over $600K up for grabs in prize pool for HBCU Students nationwide. IN 2023, the Howard University team won the $80K top prize.

Expanding Opportunities in and through Technologies

Apple worked with Southern Company and a range of community stakeholders to launch the Propel Center, a first-of-its-kind innovation and learning hub for the HBCU community. Apple's $25 million contribution that enabled the Propel Center to support HBCU students and faculty through a robust virtual platform, a physical campus in the historic Atlanta University Center, as well as on-campus activations at partner institutions is part of a $100 million pledge through the Apple Computer's Racial Equity and Justice Initiative project o challenge systemic racism, and advance racial equity nationwide:

> The concept of PROPEL was born in 2019 as a proactive solution for systemic barriers impacting HBCUs. As the United States wrestled yet again with the turmoil of social injustice and historical inequalities, companies reacted by investing in equity approaches. Yet, there was still no comprehensive solution for workforce disparities.
>
> Our journey began with a simple yet profound vision: To create enduring prosperity and improve lives through transformative educational approaches.
>
> Envisioned as an innovation hub that upskills and catapults Black talent from the HBCU ecosystem, PROPEL and founding partners Apple and Southern Company are committed to

> fostering a new generation of Black leaders via programming and workforce development.
>
> To date, we've provided over 1 million dollars in scholarships and 4 million dollars in institutional grants. In an ever-changing world, PROPEL prepares HBCU talent for the future of work, today.

PROPEL provides an **HBCU Cybersecurity Accelerator** which provides an immersive experience crafted specifically for HBCU students. Through a year-long program, students gain direct access to top-tier industry experts and cutting-edge tools, ensuring their advancement in the rapidly evolving cybersecurity industry. PROPEL also provides a Pioneering Health Accelerator Talent Program where students from various HBCUs work together on a challenge-based question. The intensive, semester-long program provides HBCU students with a multi-faceted tech skills/career development opportunity. Through this all-expense-paid program, the mission is to cultivate the next wave of skilled, industry trained and innovation-minded tech professionals committed to the development of innovative solutions, technologies, products, or services within the healthcare industry.

Apple computer also supports the Apple Developer Academy, a free 10-month program through a partnership with Michigan State University that meets at a facility in downtown Detroit:

> The Apple Developer Academy in Detroit is a partnership between MSU and Apple. Individuals 18 or older have the opportunity to become a world-class developer using Apple's IOS ecosystem. The Academy focuses on coding, design, entrepreneurship, and essential professional skills. The Apple Developer Academy offers two programs, the main Academy and Foundations, that provide learners with the opportunity to build a foundation in these domains.

On August 8, 2024, the UNCF announced that the *"UNCF and Founding HBCUs Sign Historic Agreement to Launch HBCUv, a Digital Learning and Community Engagement Platform 'By HBCUs, For HBCUs.'"*

> ATLANTA, GA, Aug. 08, 2024 (GLOBE NEWSWIRE) -- In a landmark event that promises to redefine the future of higher education, UNCF (United Negro College Fund) and six historically Black colleges and universities (HBCUs) signed a historic consortium agreement, ushering in the first official partnerships on HBCUv®. The digital learning and community engagement platform—designed by HBCUs, for HBCUs—was unveiled during UNITE 2024: UNCF Summit for Black Higher Education, marking a transformative moment for champions of Black higher education.

The schools making up the consortium are Benedict College, Clark Atlanta University, Jarvis Christian University, Lane College, Shaw University, Talladega College, Claflin University, Dillard University, and Johnson C. Smith University.

Fayetteville State University, Winston-Salem State University, and North Carolina Central University: Institute for Multi-agent Perception through Advanced Cyber-physical Technologies (IMPACT). The IMPACT project will build on existing capacity and collaboration with NASA's Jet Propulsion Laboratory in Southern California, to engage students and faculty in using data science to address scientific questions as one of the key factors to manage NASA's Earth mission research.

Florida A & M University: Effects of Gravity on Creeping Salts and Salt Mixtures: Developing Image-based and AI-enhanced Diagnostics for Determining Chemical Compositions. This project will rely on artificial intelligence and machine learning to better understand the science of concentrated salt solutions and the formation of ring-like deposits called evaporites. Understanding the science of salt concentrations and formation of evaporites will bring new insight into identifying where water may have existed. Water is a critical source NASA researches and explores to better understand other planets' surface geology and the potential future of lunar and Martian exploration.

Lincoln University (MO): Using Data Science to Understand Soil, Wildfire, & Social Disparity of Climate Change and Air Pollution. This project aims to provide data science problem-solving, skill development, and professional development of minority and underserved students. Students will utilize existing state-of-the-art ML methods to develop new data analytic approaches to solve some of the core problems in Earth science research.

NASA's new pioneering efforts to close opportunity gaps in STEM, including nearly $12 million for eight HBCUs to support programs in artificial intelligence and machine learning and create a more diverse pipeline of talent for "data-intensive space-based Earth sciences" careers: Bethune-Cookman University; Fayetteville State University; Florida A&M University; Lincoln University (MO); Morgan State University; North Carolina A&T State University; North Carolina Central University; and Prairie View A&M University.

The DoN HBCU/MI Program provides various opportunities for HBCU/MI faculty and students to collaborate with scientists and engineers at naval labs and warfare centers, on projects of mutual interest. These include student scholarships, fellowships and internships, as well as faculty summer sabbaticals as part of the Naval STEM Roadmap.

The Georgia Tech HBCU/MSI Research Collaboration Initiative is one example of the expansion of public, private, and institutional collaborations with HBCUs to greatly expand opportunities for HBCU students to pursue technology careers.

Not only do the careers reflected in the tables provide opportunities for the passionate and purposeful study of technology, they represent many different applications of technology information research scientists to video game developers. The following table reflects information collected from the U.S. Bureau of Labor Statistics Occupational Outlook Handbook, *"Computer and Information Technology Occupations"* for the array of computer and information technology occupations.

Career	**Salary**	**Description**
Computer and Information Research Scientists	$145,080	Computer and information research scientists design innovative uses for new and existing computing technology.

Career	Salary	Description
Computer Network Architects	$129,840	Computer network architects design and implement data communication networks, including local area networks (LANs), wide area networks (WANs), and intranets.
Computer Programmers	$99,700	Computer programmers write, modify, and test code and scripts that allow computer software and applications to function properly.
Computer Systems Analysts	$103,800	Computer systems analysts study an organization's current computer systems and design ways to improve efficiency.
Database Administrators and Architects	$117,450	Database administrators and architects create or organize systems to store and secure data.
Information Security Analysts	$120,360	Information security analysts plan and carry out security measures to protect an organization's computer networks and systems.
Network and Computer Systems Administrators	$95,360	Network and computer systems administrators install, configure, and maintain organizations' computer networks and systems.
Software Developers, Quality Assurance Analysts, and Testers	$130,160	Software developers design computer applications or programs. Software quality assurance analysts and testers identify problems with applications or programs and report defects.
Web Developers and Digital Designers	$92,750	Web developers create and maintain websites. Digital designers develop, create, and test website or interface layout, functions, and navigation for usability.
Video Game Designers	$91,290*	Making video games is a serious—and big—business. According to the Entertainment Software Association, in 2009, the video game industry had sales in excess of $10 billion and employed more than 32,000 people in 34 states.

Career	Salary	Description
Special Effects Artists and Animators	$99,060	Special effects artists and animators typically need a bachelor's degree in computer graphics, art, or a related field to develop both a portfolio of work and the technical skills that many employers prefer.
*Annual salary for video game designers is taken from indeed U.S. salary data.		

There are tremendous opportunities across all STEM disciplines. As HBCUs work to diversify the workforce, so too, are major corporations pursuing a similar mission as presented in Tamara Pierson's article, *"Why the most lucrative tech careers are still out of reach for so many US students."* Dr. Pearson, now a professor at Georgia Tech and former Director of the Center of Excellence for Minority Women in STEM at Spelman College, notes:

> When you look at computer science, just 8.9% of the more than 71,000 bachelor's degrees awarded in this field in 2017 went to Black students, and only 10.1% went to Latino students, federal data show. This is significantly less than the percentage of Black and Latino people in the US: 13.4% and 18.5%, respectively.
>
> The numbers are similarly bleak in the tech industry. At Google, only 9.6% of its US workforce is Black or Latino. At Apple, only 14% of its tech workforce is Black or Latino. This is particularly concerning given that those two groups make up 30% of the US labor force.

It is important to note that the two companies cited—Google and Apple—have partnerships with HBCUs to support their mission of diversifying the workplace. Apple is listed #4 and Google is listed #11 on the list of the 2024 Top 20 Industry Supporters of HBCU Engineering Schools. Apple and Google are only two of the many companies that recruit from or have forged partnerships with HBCUs.

Begin your college research for the best HBCUs for technology by performing an internet search on the phrase, "best HBCUs for technology." The search is likely to result in more results for computer science or STEM in general. Two of the results from this search are BestColleges *"Top 10 HBCUs for Computer Science Programs"* and HBCUColleges *"Top 50 HBCU computer schools."*

The reason that it is important for you to attempt to identify the specific technology major that you would like to pursue is that the opportunities for pursuing your major, as well as the opportunities for receiving scholarships to support the pursuit of your major at a specific HBCU will differ among schools.

Scholarships and Partnerships

As previously presented, beginning your scholarship search for scholarships related to your desired college major or career aspirations, and that are offered by or for HBCUS, are not only directly connected to your aspirations, but are likely to have fewer applicants than national scholarship programs open to all students.

Begin your research into HBCU-specific scholarships for technology by performing an internet search on the phrase, "hbcu technology scholarships," "scholarships for black technology majors," and "hbcu scholarships for technology majors." Expand your research to using phrases including a specific major, e.g., "hbcu scholarships for computer science majors" or "scholarships for black students majoring in engineering."

Following are some of the scholarships pertaining to technology majors and careers, some of which are only available at specific HBCUs.

Adobe Cybersecurity Internship Program: Co-created with Bowie State University as a National Center of Academic Excellence in Cyber Defense Education—helps Black students develop their cybersecurity skills to drive more diverse representation in this job area.

Accenture Level Up: Level Up will provide students from Historically Black Colleges & Universities (HBCU) and Hispanic Serving Institutions (HSI) with an environment to develop fundamental professional skills in technology and innovation while fostering the ability to build lasting relationships and career opportunities. In partnership with Microsoft, the program will work to increase the representation of technology professionals from historically underrepresented communities. If selected, students have the opportunity to complete a skill building course during the spring in preparation for an eight-week paid opportunity over the summer. Upon successful completion, students will have the chance to return as a summer intern the following year. Open to CUNY and Prairie View A&M University Sophomores, currently enrolled in a four-year undergraduate program, with no minimum GPA requirement interested in pursuing a career in technology.

Blacks at Microsoft (BAM): The BAM Scholarship was created to enable Black and African American students to attend college and pursue a career in technology. BAM will award 50 scholarships totaling $137,500 (USD). 5 awards of $5,000: Awards are renewable up to three years or until a bachelor's degree is earned, whichever occurs first, on the basis of satisfactory academic performance maintaining a cumulative grade point average of 3.0 on a 4.0 scale, full-time enrollment, and continued enrollment in the eligible major. 45 awards of $2,500: one-time only. Past recipients cannot reapply.

CodeHouse Scholars Initiative: The CodeHouse Scholars Initiative (CHSI) mentors, prepares and invests in Black, Latinx, and Native American students, in their first year of college, for a career in the tech industry. As a scholar students will be able to receive up to $20,000 academic scholarships for a tech-related degree. Must be enrolled for the first time at one of the five (5) participating HBCUs:

- Clark Atlanta University
- Howard University
- Morehouse College
- North Carolina A&T State University
- Spelman College

DoD HBCU and Minority-Serving Institution (MSI) Research and Education Program: The DoD today announced awards totaling $27 million to Historically Black Colleges and Universities (HBCUs) to conduct research in defense critical technology areas. A merit-based competition administered by the Office of Naval Research (ONR) selected three HBCUs to conduct five-year research projects in areas including artificial intelligence, machine learning, cyber security, and autonomy. The awards will enhance the capacity of the HBCUs to participate more fully in DoD research programs and activities. The funding opportunity was also designed to encourage commitments by the eligible institutions to invest time and resources that will elevate their research ranking on the Carnegie Classification of Institutions of Higher Education scale from R2 status (doctoral universities with high research activity) to R1 status (doctoral universities with very high research activity).

- **Howard University:** Building Research Capacity and Future ONR/DOD Workforce Skills In Human-Centered Artificial Intelligence at Howard University
- **Morgan State University:** Research and Education in Equitable Artificial Intelligence and Machine Learning: Cybersecurity Implications for National Defense
- **North Carolina A&T State University:** Trustworthy Cyber Physical Defense Systems via Artificial Intelligence and Shared Autonomy

DoD Smart Scholarship: The National Security Agency (NSA) and Department of Defense (DoD) offer a plethora of scholarship programs for first-year college students through graduate school. Since the National Security Agency and Department of Defense provide so many scholarship opportunities, you must visit their respective websites to identify programs that align with your college major or career aspirations.

Fontana Transport Inc. Scholars Program: Open to first generation high school seniors who are underrepresented, need financial assistance and are passionate about furthering their education as a means to help out their family, community and themselves. Candidates must be planning to study: Transportation

Management; Math; Science; Engineering (any field); Architecture; Environmental Design; Premed; Psychology; or Spanish Language/ Literature.

Fossi Scholarship: $40K scholarship awarded to a high school student planning to attend an HBCU and major in Science, Technology, Engineering, or Math. Not intended for students interested in pursuing careers in nursing, medicine, psychology, social sciences and other associated fields. Some fields of study which may be considered STEM may not qualify for FOSSI scholarships.

Fund II Foundation UNCF STEM Scholars Program: Applicants must be African American, full-time, first-year students with demonstrated unmet financial need. They must have completed advanced math and science courses in high school, including pre-calculus. This scholarship is specifically for students intending to pursue science, technology, mathematics, or engineering (STEM) majors.

Google In Residence: The Google in Residence (GIR) program was created to support greater diversity in the tech industry. In partnership with computer science departments at Historically Black Colleges and Universities (HBCUs) and Hispanic Serving Institutions (HSIs), Googlers—experienced software engineers—spend the fall semester (August-December) on campuses, teaching introductory computer science classes. First-year students learn about basic coding and debugging, simple data structures, and how to work with large code bases. They also gain practical knowledge about what it's like to work in the tech industry and what development is like in a team.

Partner HBCUs:

- Alabama A&M
- Fisk University
- Hampton University
- Morehouse College
- Morgan State University

- North Carolina A&T State University
- Prairie View A&M University
- Tennessee State University
- Xavier University of Louisiana

IBM Cybersecurity Talent Initiative: IBM is collaborating with the 20 HBCUs to co-create Cybersecurity Leadership Centers, helping to create talent for employers and opportunities for students.

Partner HBCUs:

- Alabama A&M University
- Albany State University
- Alcorn State University
- Bowie State University
- Clark Atlanta University
- Edward Waters University
- Florida A&M University
- Grambling State University
- Morgan State University
- Norfolk State University
- North Carolina A&T State University
- North Carolina Central University
- South Carolina State University
- Southern University and A&M College
- Talladega College
- Texas Southern University
- Tuskegee University
- Voorhees University
- West Virginia State University
- Xavier University of Louisiana

IBM Quantum education and research initiative for Historically Black Colleges and Universities (HBCU): Led by Howard University and 12 additional HBCUs, the IBM-HBCU Quantum Center will offer access to its quantum computers, as well as collaboration on academic, education, and community outreach programs. The IBM-HBCU Quantum Center is a multi-year investment designed to prepare and develop talent at HBCUs from all STEM disciplines for the quantum future. The 13 HBCUs intending to participate in the Quantum Center were prioritized based on their research and education focus in physics, engineering, mathematics, computer science, and other STEM fields.

Partner HBCUs:

- Albany State University
- Clark Atlanta University
- Coppin State University
- Hampton University
- Howard University
- Morehouse College
- Morgan State University
- North Carolina A&T State University
- Southern University
- Texas Southern University
- University of the Virgin Islands
- Virginia Union University
- Xavier University of Louisiana

Intel Scholars Program: Intel is committed to helping create a better world and having a positive impact on global social challenges by supporting underrepresented groups on their path to becoming the next generation of innovators. The Intel Scholars program aims to expand access and opportunity, and to increase the pipeline of diverse STEM talent, by providing nearly $2 million annually to African American, Latinx, Native American, women and veteran STEM students through hundreds of higher education scholarships.

José E. Serrano Educational Partnership Program with Minority Serving Institutions: Open to rising college juniors majoring in Science, Technology, Engineering, or Mathematics (STEM) at Minority Serving Institutions.

KnowBe4 Black Americans in Cybersecurity (U.S.): Offers a yearly $10,000 scholarship, which is open to any American of Black heritage who is currently pursuing a degree in cybersecurity.

Medtronic Leadership Development Program: The program creates capacity-building opportunities through its Research and Development program which supports innovation and innovative solutions in STEM across HBCUs for underrepresented students pursuing engineering, biomedical, and business at Historically Black Colleges and Universities (HBCUs) across the U.S.

NASA: Closing opportunity gaps in STEM by providing nearly $12 million for eight HBCUs to support programs in artificial intelligence and machine learning and create a more diverse pipeline of talent for "data-intensive space-based Earth sciences" careers:

- Bethune-Cookman University
- Fayetteville State University
- Florida A&M University
- Lincoln University (MO)
- Morgan State University
- North Carolina A&T State University
- North Carolina Central University
- Prairie View A&M University

NASA - Advancing STEM At Minority-Serving Institutions: The Minority University Research and Education Project (MUREP) is administered through NASA's Office of STEM Engagement. Through MUREP, NASA provides financial assistance via competitive awards to Minority Serving Institutions, including Historically Black Colleges and Universities, Hispanic Serving Institutions, Asian American and Native American Pacific Islander Serving Institutions, Alaska Native and Native Hawaiian-Serving Institutions, American

Indian Tribal Colleges and Universities, Native American-Serving Nontribal Institutions and other MSIs, as required by the MSI-focused Executive Orders. These institutions recruit and retain underrepresented and underserved students, including women and girls, and persons with disabilities, into science, technology, engineering and mathematics (STEM) fields.

Naval STEM: Naval Science, Technology, Engineering and Mathematics (STEM) supports the Department of the Navy (DoN)'s Navy and Marine Corps education and outreach programs. Naval STEM programs are deliberate investments in the current and future DoN workforce, which enhance the Navy and Marine Corps' ability to meet present and future war-fighting challenges.

- **Junior Science and Humanities Symposium (JSHS) Program:** JSHS is a tri-service – U.S. Navy, Army, and Air Force-sponsored competition which promotes original research and experimentation in STEM at the high school level. JSHS aims to widen the pool of trained talent prepared to conduct research and development vital to our nation. *Website: JSHS.org*
- **National Defense Science & Engineering Graduate (NDSEG):** NDSEG provides fellowships to support study and research leading to doctoral degrees in science and technical areas. NDSEG confers high honors upon its recipients, and allows them to attend whichever U.S. institution they choose. *Website: ndseg.sysplus.com/*
- **Naval Research Enterprise Internship Program (NREIP):** NREIP is a 10-week undergraduate and graduate research internship opportunity at one of nearly 30 naval laboratories or warfare centers. Accepted students gain real-world, hands-on experience and research skills while being introduced to the Navy and Marine Corps science and technology environment. *Website: navalsteminterns.us/nreip*
- **Naval Science Awards Program (NSAP):** NSAP is a U.S. Navy and Marine Corps program that encourages students to develop and retain an interest in STEM. NSAP recognizes the accomplishments of eligible students at regional and

state science and engineering fairs and the International Science and Engineering Fair (ISEF) in producing quality science and engineering projects. *Website: onr.navy.mil/Education-Outreach/K-12-Programs/NSAP*

- **Science and Engineering Apprenticeship Program (SEAP):** SEAP is an 8-week high school apprenticeship opportunity at one of nearly 25 naval laboratories or warfare centers. Accepted students gain real-world, hands-on experience and research skills while being introduced to the Navy and Marine Corps science and technology environment. *Website: navalsteminterns.us/seap/*
- **Science, Mathematics & Research for Transformation (SMART):** SMART Scholarship for Service Program is an opportunity for students pursuing an undergraduate or graduate degree in STEM disciplines to receive a full scholarship and be gainfully employed upon degree completion. *Website: smartscholarship.org/smart*

PG&E Better Together STEM Scholarships: Pacific Gas and Electric Company (PG&E) Foundation is offering Better Together STEM Scholarships of $2,500, $5,000 or $10,000. These are for students pursuing science, technology or engineering studies who plan to enroll as a full-time undergraduate student in an eligible STEM field at any accredited four-year college or university in California or a Historical Black College or University (HBCU) for the entire upcoming academic year.

Playstation Career Pathways: PlayStation Career Pathways is designed to provide participants (Pathways Scholars) with access, opportunity, education and exposure to gaming careers and to the gaming industry. The multi-year program provides. Each Pathways Scholar receives a scholarship in the amount of $30k to help offset the cost of their university education. Students may learn more and apply through UNCF, Jackie Robinson Foundation, and USC-Games.

To research other scholarships, begin with the listing of top industry supporters, government and nonprofit supporters, and top employers. Perform an internet search on the phrase "name of company + scholarships," "name of company + hbcu scholarships," and "name of company + scholarships for black students."

Resources

Associations and networking organizations for technology:

- AllStarCode
- Benjamin Banneker Association
- Black & Brown Founders
- Black Boys Code
- Black Code Collective
- Black Data Processing Associates
- Black Founders
- Black Girls Code
- Black Professionals in Tech Network
- Black Tech Nation
- Black Tech Pipeline
- Black Women Talk Tech
- BlackComputerHER
- Blacks in Technology
- Blacks United in Leading Technology International
- ChickTech
- Code Black Indy
- Code2040
- Coding Black Females
- Coffee & Coded
- ColorStack
- DevColor
- DigitalUndivided
- Django Girls

- Dream Corps Tech
- Enhancing Diversity in Graduate Education
- Girls Develop It
- Girls Who Code
- Hidden Genius Project
- Information Technology Senior Management Forum
- Informs
- National Association of Black STEM Teachers
- National Alliance for Inclusive & Diverse STEM Faculty
- National Girls Collaborative Project
- National Society of Blacks in Computing
- Nonprofit Technology Enterprise Network
- Opportunity Hub
- ProActive Network
- Technologists of Color
- Teens Exploring Technology
- The Algebra Project
- The Knowledge House
- We Build Black
- WonderWomenTech
- Young People's Project

HBCU Engineering Pathways

HBCUs are hubs for pursuing engineering degrees in and through HBCUs. Many HBCUs offer dual degree programs for earning two undergraduate degrees, while other HBCUs offer dual degree programs for earning a bachelor's degree at an HBCU and earning a master's degree at such schools as Caltech, Georgia Tech, Clemson, and Case Western Reserve.

The following table reflects information collected from the U.S. Bureau of Labor Statistics Occupational Outlook Handbook, *"Architecture and Engineering Occupations,"* for the array of science related careers.

Career	Salary	Description
Aerospace Engineering and Operations Technologists and Technicians	$77,830	Aerospace engineering and operations technologists and technicians run and maintain equipment used to develop, test, produce, and sustain aircraft and spacecraft.
Aerospace Engineers	$130,720	Aerospace engineers design, develop, and test aircraft, spacecraft, satellites, and missiles.
Agricultural Engineers	$88,750	Agricultural engineers solve problems concerning power supplies, machine efficiency, the use of structures and facilities, pollution and environmental issues, and the storage and processing of agricultural products.

Career	Salary	Description
Architects	$93,310	Architects plan and design houses, factories, office buildings, and other structures.
Bioengineers and Biomedical Engineers	$100,730	Bioengineers and biomedical engineers combine engineering principles with sciences to design and create equipment, devices, computer systems, and software.
Cartographers and Photogrammetrists	$76,210	Cartographers and photogrammetrists collect, analyze, and interpret geographic information to create and update maps and related products.
Chemical Engineers	$112,100	Chemical engineers apply the principles of chemistry, physics, and engineering to design equipment and processes for manufacturing products such as gasoline, detergents, and paper.
Civil Engineers	$95,890	Civil engineers plan, design, and supervise the construction and maintenance of building and infrastructure projects.
Computer Hardware Engineers	$138,080	Computer hardware engineers research, design, develop, and test computer systems and components.
Electrical and Electronics Engineers	$109,010	Electrical engineers design, develop, test, and supervise the manufacture of electrical equipment.
Environmental Engineers	$100,090	Environmental engineers use engineering disciplines in developing solutions to problems of planetary health.

Career	Salary	Description
Health and Safety Engineers	$103,690	Health and safety engineers combine knowledge of engineering and of health and safety to develop procedures and design systems to protect people from illness and injury and property from damage.
Industrial Engineers	$99,380	Industrial engineers design, develop, and test integrated systems for managing industrial production processes.
Marine Engineers and Naval Architects	$100,270	Marine engineers and naval architects design, build, and maintain ships, from aircraft carriers to submarines and from sailboats to tankers.
Materials Engineers	$104,100	Materials engineers develop, process, and test materials used to create a wide range of products.
Mechanical Engineers	$99,510	Mechanical engineers design, develop, build, and test mechanical and thermal sensors and devices.
Mining and Geological Engineers	$100,640	Mining and geological engineers design mines to safely and efficiently remove minerals for use in manufacturing and utilities.
Nuclear Engineers	$125,460	Nuclear engineers research and develop projects or address problems concerning the release, control, and use of nuclear energy and nuclear waste disposal.
Petroleum Engineers	$135,690	Petroleum engineers devise methods to improve oil and gas extraction and production.

Through federal grants and private sector partnerships, students have opportunities to explore a broad range of engineering career pathways.

Self-Driving Vehicles: North Carolina A&T State University received a $550K grant from the National Science Foundation (NSF) and a $235K grant from the North Carolina Department of Transportation (NCDOT) to establish a Testbed of Connected Autonomous MicroTransit Vehicles. Since receiving the grant in 2020, the school has developed the "Aggie Auto Shuttles" to develop better transportation choices in rural areas as well as connecting places that have little to no access to public transportation. The partnership has grown to include the U.S. Department of Transportation, U.S. Federal Highway Administration, Google, Verizon, Volvo, Intel, RTI, and the city of Greensboro, NC.

Prairie View A&M University opened a $70 million state-of-the-art engineering building.

The CNN Business article previously cited, *"Major companies are recruiting more HBCU grads than ever before, administrators say"* also notes:

> The median full-time starting salary for Howard grads is now about $72,680, according to the school's latest exit survey for graduating students.
>
> Howard says JPMorgan Chase (JPM), Deloitte, Procter & Gamble (PG), Goldman Sachs and McKinsey & Co. rank among the top 25 companies that recruit at the university. That list also includes Accenture (ACN), Microsoft (MSFT), Facebook (FB), Apple and Google (GOOG), which has a tech partnership with the school.
>
> The added corporate engagement for Howard has helped it recruit more high school graduates and increase enrollment, according to Howard University provost Anthony Wutoh.
>
> "In my 25-year experience with Howard University, this is the most significant interest that I've seen corporations demonstrate in Howard students," Wutoh told CNN Business on Monday. "Our efforts to build partnerships and programs that

benefit Howard students have led us to this unprecedented time in history where even more corporations are realizing the value of a Howard education."

HBCUs offer math and science competitions:

- The HBCU Battle of the Brains
- NASA's MITTIC Competition
- HBCU C2
- DoE HBCU Clean Energy Education Prize
- U.S. Army xTech HBCU Competition
- Honda Campus All Star Challenge
- HBCU Tech Conference
- HBCU & HSI National Supply Chain Case Competition

Scholarships and Partnerships

As previously presented, beginning your scholarship search for scholarships related to your desired college major or career aspirations, and that are offered by or for HBCUS, are not only directly connected to your aspirations, but are likely to have fewer applicants than national scholarship programs open to all students.

Begin your research into HBCU-specific scholarships for technology by performing an internet search on the phrase, "hbcu technology scholarships," "scholarships for black technology majors," and "hbcu scholarships for technology majors." Expand your research to using phrases including a specific major, e.g., "hbcu scholarships for computer science majors" or "scholarships for black students majoring in engineering."

Following are some of the scholarships pertaining to technology majors and careers, some of which are only available at specific HBCUs.

Advancing Minorities' Interest in Engineering (AMIE): Advancing Minorities' Interest in Engineering (AMIE) is a non-profit organization whose purpose is to expand corporate and government alliances with the (17) ABET accredited Historically Black Colleges and Universities (HBCU) Schools of Engineering to implement and support programs to attract, educate, graduate and place underrepresented minority students in engineering and computer science careers. The (16) ABET accredited HBCU Schools of Engineering produce 30% of the African American engineers in the United States while representing 3% of the Engineering Universities. Approximately one-third of African American graduates in Science and Engineering are also produced by Historically Black Colleges and Universities (HBCU). One quarter of PhD recipients in Science and Engineering received their undergraduate degree from Historically Black Colleges and Universities (HBCU).

Partner HBCUs:

- Alabama A&M University
- Central State University
- Florida A&M University
- Hampton University
- Howard University
- Jackson State University
- Morgan State University
- Norfolk State University
- North Carolina A&T State University
- Prairie View A&M University
- Southern University and A&M College
- Tennessee State University
- Texas Southern University

- Tuskegee University
- University of Maryland Eastern Shore
- University of the District of Columbia
- Virginia State University

Amazon Future Engineer Scholarship: Be a high school senior in the U.S. who is currently enrolled in or who has completed a high school or college dual degree course where computer science, engineering, or robotics is the subject. Students who have not taken this course can opt-in to take an assessment offered by Amazon.

Apple HBCU Scholars Program: Selected scholars will receive a $15,000 merit-based scholarship and participate in a 12-week internship during the Summer of 2024. Each scholar will be assigned an Apple mentor throughout their experience, receive an opportunity to develop key skills, and help launch their careers through the hands-on experience gained at one of the most innovative tech companies in the world.

Baxter STEM Scholars Program: The Thurgood Marshall College Fund (TMCF) and Baxter International Foundation are proud to offer financial assistance to outstanding African American and/or African descent STEM majors attending Historically Black Colleges and Universities (HBCUs) and Predominantly Black Institutions (PBIs). Forty scholars will be selected to receive a fall need-based scholarship up to $20,000 for the academic school year. Student must be enrolled full-time as a sophomore at a school listed below:

- Hampton University
- Howard University
- Norfolk State University
- Spelman College
- Xavier University of Louisiana

BP HBCU Fellowship Program: As part of BP's HBCU Fellowship Program, 3 HBCUs received $1.35 million each, covering five full scholarships per year at each school for three years—a total of 45 full scholarships. Students who successfully complete the program are provided with opportunities for additional development, including internships:

- Florida A&M University
- North Carolina A&T State University
- Prairie View A&M University

Boeing - TMCF Scholar Program: Provides students with full college-to-career support—opening the door to a full-time career with the world's largest aerospace company, and lead manufacturer of commercial jetliners and defense, space and security systems.

BRPH Future Achievers Scholarship: Architecture or engineering majors at the following HBCUs:

- Florida A&M University
- Tuskegee University

Chairish Design Your Future Scholarship: Open to all students, with preference given to students from underrepresented backgrounds in design and engineering majors.

Deloitte HBCU Emerging Leaders Scholarship Program: Deloitte Foundation funds scholarships for HBCU undergraduate students majoring in accounting, business, and STEM to help build pathways to opportunity and diversify the workforce in these fields. This program will give you first-hand exposure to the professional services industry, allowing you to learn new business skills and deepen your knowledge in your field of interest. You will also have the opportunity to build a professional network across different business areas within Deloitte. Applicants will participate in virtual interviews to be considered for internships and employment opportunities. The interviews will include an assessment of the applicant's leadership skills demonstrating strong judgment, problem-solving, and decision-making abilities. Those who receive an internship or full-time job offer will be eligible to attend the Deloitte HBCU Emerging Leaders Scholarship Program. Eligible participants will compete at Deloitte University or virtually to be considered for a Deloitte HBCU Emerging Leaders Scholarship of $10,000.

To research other scholarships, begin with the listing of top industry supporters, government and nonprofit supporters, and top employers. Perform an internet search on the phrase "name of company + scholarships," "name of company + hbcu scholarships," and "name of company + scholarships for black students."

Resources

Associations and networking organizations for engineering:

- American Academy of Environmental Engineers & Scientists
- American Institute of Aeronautics and Astronautics
- American Institute of Chemical Engineers
- American Institute of Mining, Metallurgical, and Petroleum Engineers
- American Society for Engineering Education
- American Society of Civil Engineers
- American Society of Heating, Refrigerating and Air-Conditioning Engineers
- American Society of Mechanical Engineers
- Association of Computing Machinery
- Biomedical Engineering Society
- Black Professionals in STEM
- Black Women in Science & Engineering
- Enhancing Diversity in Graduate Education
- Harvard Society of Black Scientists and Engineers
- Hidden Genius Project
- IEEE Power & Energy Society
- Institute for Biological Engineering
- Institute of Electrical and Electronics Engineers
- Institute of Industrial & Systems Engineers
- Institute of Transportation Engineers
- International Academy for Production Engineering
- National Academies of Sciences Engineering and Medicine
- National Academy of Engineering
- National Action Council for Minorities in Engineering

- National Association of Black STEM Teachers
- National Association of Multicultural Engineering
- National Center for Women & Information Technology
- National Council of Structural Engineers Association
- National Organization for the Professional Advancement of Black Chemists and Chemical Engineers
- National Science Foundation
- National Science Foundation Mathematical Sciences Institutes
- National Society of Black Engineers
- National Society of Black Engineers Summer Engineering Experience
- National Society of Professional Engineers
- Nonprofit Technology Enterprise Network
- Opportunity Hub
- ProActive Network
- Science Robotics
- Society of Automotive Engineers
- Society of Manufacturing Engineers
- Society of Women Engineers
- Tapia Center for Excellence and Equity in Education
- Teens Exploring Technology
- Technologists of Color
- The Algebra Project
- The Knowledge House
- We Build Black
- Women in Engineering
- WonderWomenTech
- Young People's Project

HBCU Math Pathways

While I have worked with many Black students who not only had a love for learning math, but who developed such deep levels of math knowledge, they were able to earn top scores on the SAT and ACT math sections. However, only two of these students affirmed pursuing a math-related PhD. Kimberly who received her BA in Math and Chemistry from Williams College is completing her PhD in Math at Iowa State University. Sam, who was a Meyerhoff Scholar at the University of Maryland - Baltimore County is completing his PhD in Economics at Oxford University in English. In part, due to the body of work developed by each student in math and economics, Sam is a Rhodes Scholar and Kimberly is a National Science Foundation Graduate Fellow.

With these two exceptions, nearly all of the students with whom I have worked who had a passion for mathematics chose to pursue healthcare career pathways. The research study, *"Cultivating and leveraging the community cultural wealth of Black students in high cognitive demand elementary mathematics classrooms,"* provides insight into why so few Black students may be pursuing careers in the mathematical sciences:

> Community cultural wealth (CCW) is shown to play a role in the STEM persistence of Black students. White teachers often view their Black students through a deficit-based lens and may struggle to recognize and access the CCW of their nonwhite students.
>
> In the US, approximately 80% of public elementary and secondary mathematics teachers are White, and Black students are likely to have White mathematics teachers throughout the majority of their K-12 schooling. Even in schools with majority Black student populations, White educators make up 54% percent of classroom teachers. Unfortunately, White teachers tend to have more negative perceptions of their Black students compared to students of other races (McGrady & Reynolds, 2013; Malone et al., 2023; Quinn & Stewart, 2019).

Whether or not these reflect your experiences in your K-12 math classes, Noelle Sawyer, a Bahamian mathematician shares her experience in During the first two years of her undergraduate program, Sawyer, whose research focuses on dynamics and geometry, kept wondering, "Why is no one treating me like I'm good at learning things?"

> Marissa Kawehi Loving is a National Science Foundation postdoctoral researcher and a visiting assistant mathematics professor at the Georgia Institute of Technology and co-founder of the Web site Indigenous Mathematicians. When Loving, whose research focuses on low-dimensional topology and geometric group theory, was in graduate school, she says, she "felt like I literally couldn't win." If she accomplished something, she adds, either no one acknowledged it or they would say that "I only got that really, really good thing because of my identity and not because of my talent." Even though Sawyer is now an assistant professor, she says that she still encounters other mathematicians who treat her as if she does not belong. "I hate going to conferences because someone says something hurtful or harmful to me almost every time,"

Blacks only make up 9% of the math workforce, which, while highly underrepresented, is higher than Black representation in engineering (5%), computers (7%), physical science (6%), and life science (6%). (Source: Temming 4/14/21)

The following table reflects information collected from the U.S. Bureau of Labor Statistics Occupational Outlook Handbook, *"Math Occupations,"* for the array of math related careers.

Career	Salary	Description
Actuaries	$120,000	Actuaries use mathematics, statistics, and financial theory to analyze the economic costs of risk and uncertainty.
Data Scientists	$108,020	Data scientists use analytical tools and techniques to extract meaningful insights from data.
Mathematicians and Statisticians	$104,860	Mathematicians and statisticians analyze data and apply computational techniques to solve problems.
Operations Research Analysts	$83,640	Operations research analysts use mathematics and logic to help solve complex issues.
Computer and Information Systems	$169,510	Computer and information systems managers plan, coordinate, and direct computer-related activities in an organization.
Management Analysts	$99,410	Management analysts recommend ways to improve an organization's efficiency.
Elementary School Teachers	$63,680	Kindergarten and elementary school teachers instruct young students in basic subjects in order to prepare them for future schooling.
Secondary School Teachers	$65,220	High school teachers teach academic lessons and various skills that students will need to attend college and to enter the job market.

Beyond the jobs reflected in the previous table, math is used across STEM disciplines and across a wide range of occupations, including:

Aeronautical Engineers Algorithm Engineers Certified Public Accountants Civil Engineers Chemists Economists Financial Analysts	Financial Modelers Insurance Underwriters Investment Analysts Mechanical Engineers Purchasing Managers Robotics Engineers Treasurers

Begin your college research for the best HBCUs for mathematics by performing an internet search on the phrase, "best HBCUs for math." The search is likely to result in more results for STEM in general, so you can change the phrase to "best HBCUs for + career or major, " e.g., best HBCUs for actuaries. Your search will eventually reveal Morgan State University, the only HBCU to offer a degree in Actuarial Science. The program is also supported by a scholarship program with Symetra Life Insurance. Your internet search is unlikely to result in a link to Dillard University, which offers a BS in Mathematics and Actuarial Science. Dillard University, like many HBCUs, offers programs that are difficult to find unless you go to the school's website.

Symetra Scholarship Program in Actuarial Science: Morgan State University announced a partnership with Symetra Life Insurance to provide $750,000 in scholarships supporting 25 MSU scholars pursuing a degree in actuarial science. The scholarship program is part of Symetra's national commitment to promote diversity in opportunities and outcomes for students, by teaming with HBCUs. The scholarship program will provide wraparound support for critical student needs, such as housing, food, clothing, transportation, and other emergency funding that may be a barrier to degree completion. Morgan is the only HBCU in the nation, and one of two institutions in the state of Maryland, to offer a bachelor's degree in actuarial science.

If you are passionate about math, repeat this process and explore various types of careers in mathematics.

Scholarships and Partnerships

Since math is frequently considered under the umbrella of STEM, you may experience challenges with identifying specific HBCU-specific scholarships pertaining to math. Begin your search for scholarships sponsored by a specific company on the UNCF and TMCF websites by performing an internet search on the phrase

- site: uncf.org stem scholarships **[site: + uncf.org + name of company + scholarships]** limits the search to UNCF-affiliated scholarships or scholarships posted on the UNCF website.
- site: tmcf.org stem scholarships **[site: + tmcf.org + name of company + scholarships]** limits the search to TMCF-affiliated scholarships or scholarships posted on the TMCF website.
- you can also perform a scholarship search on each website specifically for math **[site: + tmcf.org + math + scholarships]** and **[site: + uncf.org + math + scholarships]** with the exact phrase as (site: uncf.org math scholarships) and (site: tmcf.org math scholarships).

Performing an broader internet search on the phrase, "scholarships for mathematicians" will yield such results as:

- Top 170 Math Scholarships at Scholarships360
- Mathematics Scholarships at Scholarships.com
- 148 Scholarships for Mathematics Majors at SmartScholar
- Math Scholarships for College and STEM Students at Unigo

Resources

Governing boards, associations, and networking organizations for math:

- American Academy of Arts and Sciences
- American Association of University Women
- American Mathematical Society
- American Statistical Association
- Association for Women in Mathematics

- Benjamin Banneker Association
- Black & Brown Founders
- Black Girls Love Math
- Black Girls Who Math
- Black Math Collective
- Black Professionals in STEM
- Blacks in Mathematics Association
- Bridge to Enter Advanced Mathematics
- Center for Minorities in the Mathematical Sciences
- Conference for African American Researchers in the Mathematical Sciences
- Enhancing Diversity in Graduate Education
- Erikson Institute Early Math Collaborative
- Hidden Genius Project
- Indigenous Mathematics
- Institute for Advanced Study Women+ and Mathematics
- Mathematical Association of America
- Mathematically Gifted and Black
- Mathematicians of the African Diaspora
- MEETaMathematician
- National Academies
- National Alliance for Inclusive & Diverse STEM Faculty
- National Association of Black STEM Teachers
- National Association of Mathematicians
- National Science Foundation Mathematical Sciences Institutes
- Society for Industrial and Applied Mathematics
- Tapia Center for Excellence and Equity in Education
- Teens Exploring Technology
- Technologists of Color
- The Algebra Project
- The Knowledge House
- We Build Black
- Young People's Project

Dual Degree Programs

Graduate school opportunities vary widely by college: some colleges offer dual degree programs in their college or through partnerships with other schools; some colleges offer guaranteed graduate school, medical school, or law school admissions; and some colleges have a track record of their students gaining admission into top graduate school programs.

When evaluating dual degree programs, it is important to be mindful of:

- Earning a higher salary as a result of receiving 2 degrees.
- Earning 2 degrees in less time, which reduces college costs.
- Having a guaranteed pathway through 2 institutions.

You must also be mindful of researching these programs early enough in your college-planning process to meet the program requirements.

Dual degree programs may offer 2 undergraduate degrees from 2 different institutions or a bachelor's degree from one institution and a master's degree from another institution. Following are some of the types of dual degree programs in STEM. After reviewing the following examples, refer to the tables for a comprehensive listing of HBCU dual degree program opportunities.

Dillard — Georgia Tech: The Physics program offers a unique opportunity for students to pursue a dual degree (BS/BE) in collaboration with esteemed institutions such as Columbia University, Georgia Institute of Technology, Tulane University, and University of New Orleans. With a comprehensive curriculum spanning 137 credit hours, including 52 credit hours of major requirements and 20 credit hours of additional coursework, students acquire the necessary skills and knowledge for success in their chosen fields.

Fayetteville State — North Carolina State: Fayetteville State University and North Carolina State University offer "3 + 2" Dual Degree Programs. Students can earn two Bachelor of Science degrees in about 5 years-a BS in Chemistry, Computer Science or Mathematics at FSU and a BS in Chemical Engineering, Computer Engineering, Electrical Engineering or Civil Engineering from NCSU.

Fisk — Vanderbilt: The Fisk/Vanderbilt Dual Degree program allows a student to earn both a Bachelor's Degree from Fisk with a science major (Biology, Chemistry, Math and Computer Science and Physics) plus Bachelor's Degree from Vanderbilt University in Biomedical Engineering, Chemical Engineering, Civil Engineering, Computer Engineering, Computer Science, Electrical Engineering or Mechanical Engineering. This is a five year program, with the first three years spent in residence at Fisk and the last two years spent living on the Vanderbilt campus.

Fisk — Case Western Reserve: The Program is a "three + two" Dual Degree Program between Fisk University and Case Western Reserve University, leading to a Bachelor of Arts (BA) or Bachelor of Science (BS) degree in Biology, Chemistry, Computer Science, Mathematics and Physics from Fisk and a Bachelor of Science in Engineering degree from Case.

Fort Valley State — Multiple Institutions: The FVSU-CDEP program has established 3+2 dual-degree programs with Georgia Tech (GT), the University of Nevada, Las Vegas (UNLV), Penn State University (PSU), the University of Texas-Austin (UT-Austin), the University of Texas Pan American (UTPA), and the University of Arkansas (UARK). The dual-degree programs operate by students enrolling for three years at FVSU and majoring in mathematics, chemistry or biology and then transferring to a partnering institution to continue their second degree option. After successful completion of both programs, students will receive two Bachelor of Science degrees: one degree from FVSU and the second degree from a collaborating university.

Spelman College — University of Michigan: This program provides an accelerated path to a Master of Science degree in three Michigan Public Health Programs: Biostatistics, Environmental Health Sciences and Nutritional Sciences. Students who complete and graduate from this program will receive a bachelor's degree from Spelman College and a master's degree from the University of Michigan.

Xavier University of Louisiana — Various Schools: The Xavier University Dual Degree Engineering Program is designed to give a solid academic background in the sciences and mathematics that are essential to persons who are interested in becoming engineers. Xavier currently has agreements with the following Engineering Schools: Georgia Institute of Technology, Louisiana State University, North Carolina A&T State University, Notre-Dame University, Southern University at Baton Rouge, University of Detroit Mercy, University of New Orleans, and University of Wisconsin-Madison.

After reviewing the tables, and to identify the most currently available information, visit each college's website or perform an Internet search on the phrase "college name + dual degree program" to identify dual degree opportunities such as the 4-1 (Public Health) program between Claflin University and the University of South Carolina or opportunities such as the 3-2 (Physics and Electrical Engineering) program between North Carolina Central University and North Carolina State University.

Program	HBCU	Summary
Auburn University	Clark Atlanta University Spelman College Morehouse College	The Dual Degree Engineering Program (DDEP) is a cooperative arrangement with the Atlanta University Center (i.e. Clark Atlanta University, Spelman College, and Morehouse College) Consortium and 15 partner engineering institutions.
Caltech	Spelman College	The Dual Degree Engineering Program (DDEP) is a cooperative arrangement with Spelman College.
Case Western Reserve University School Engineering	Fisk University	The Program is a "three + two" Dual Degree Program between Fisk University and Case Western Reserve University, leading to a Bachelor of Arts (BA) or Bachelor of Science (BS) degree in Biology, Chemistry, Computer Science, Mathematics and Physics from Fisk and a Bachelor of Science in Engineering degree from Case. Dual Degree Students can major in the following disciplines at Case Western Reserve University School of Engineering: • Aerospace Engineering • Biomedical Engineering • Chemical Engineering • Civil Engineering • Computer Engineering
Clarkson University	Morehouse College	Since 1969, Morehouse College has offered students the option of studying engineering through the dual-degree engineering program, which consists of cooperative agreements with a number of engineering schools.
Clemson University Dual Engineering Degree	Claflin University	After three years, successful students may transfer to Clemson to finish the degree requirements for one of Clemson's 11 Engineering Bachelor's degrees[1]. Upon completion of the Engineering degree at Clemson, students are awarded a B.S. degree in their Engineering major from Clemson and a B.A. or B.S. degree from their original partner school.

Program	HBCU	Summary
Columbia University	Dillard University Spelman College Morehouse College	The Dual Degree Engineering Program (DDEP) is a cooperative arrangement with the Atlanta University Center (i.e. Clark Atlanta University, Spelman College, and Morehouse College) Consortium and 15 partner engineering institutions.
Dartmouth College	Spelman College Morehouse College	The Dual Degree Engineering Program (DDEP) is a cooperative arrangement with Spelman College and Morehouse College.
Georgia Tech	Dillard University Fort Valley State University Xavier University of Louisiana	The FVSU-CDEP program has established 3+2 dual-degree programs with Georgia Tech (GT), the University of Nevada, Las Vegas (UNLV), Penn State University (PSU), the University of Texas-Austin (UT-Austin), the University of Texas Pan American (UTPA), and the University of Arkansas (UARK).
Georgia Tech	Clark Atlanta University Dillard University Spelman College Morehouse College Xavier University of Louisiana	The Dual Degree Engineering Program (DDEP) is a cooperative arrangement with the Atlanta University Center (i.e. Clark Atlanta University, Spelman College, and Morehouse College) Consortium and 15 partner engineering institutions.
Indiana University - Purdue University Indianapolis	Clark Atlanta University Spelman College Morehouse College	The Dual Degree Engineering Program (DDEP) is a cooperative arrangement with the Atlanta University Center (i.e. Clark Atlanta University, Spelman College, and Morehouse College) Consortium and 15 partner engineering institutions.

Program	HBCU	Summary
Louisiana State University	Xavier University of Louisiana	The Xavier University Dual Degree Engineering Program is designed to give a solid academic background in the sciences and mathematics that are essential to persons who are interested in becoming engineers.
North Carolina A&T State University	Xavier University of Louisiana	The Xavier University Dual Degree Engineering Program is designed to give a solid academic background in the sciences and mathematics that are essential to persons who are interested in becoming engineers.
North Carolina A&T State University	Clark Atlanta University Spelman College Morehouse College	The Dual Degree Engineering Program (DDEP) is a cooperative arrangement with the Atlanta University Center (i.e. Clark Atlanta University, Spelman College, and Morehouse College) Consortium and 15 partner engineering institutions.
North Carolina State University	Fayetteville State University	Fayetteville State University and North Carolina State University offer "3 + 2" Dual Degree Programs. Students can earn two Bachelor of Science degrees in about 5 years-a BS in Chemistry, Computer Science or Mathematics at FSU and a BS in Chemical Engineering, Computer Engineering, Electrical Engineering or Civil Engineering from NCSU.
Penn State University	Fort Valley State University	The FVSU-CDEP program has established a 3+2 dual-degree program with Penn State University (PSU).
Rensselaer Polytechnic University	Clark Atlanta University Spelman College Morehouse College	The Dual Degree Engineering Program (DDEP) is a cooperative arrangement with the Atlanta University Center (i.e. Clark Atlanta University, Spelman College, and Morehouse College) Consortium and 15 partner engineering institutions.

Program	HBCU	Summary
Rochester Institute of Technology	Clark Atlanta University Spelman College Morehouse College	The Dual Degree Engineering Program (DDEP) is a cooperative arrangement with the Atlanta University Center (i.e. Clark Atlanta University, Spelman College, and Morehouse College) Consortium and 15 partner engineering institutions.
Southern University at Baton Rouge	Xavier University of Louisiana	The Xavier University Dual Degree Engineering Program is designed to give a solid academic background in the sciences and mathematics that are essential to persons who are interested in becoming engineers.
University of Alabama - Huntsville	Morehouse College	Since 1969, Morehouse College has offered students the option of studying engineering through the dual-degree engineering program, which consists of cooperative agreements with a number of engineering schools.
University of Arkansas (UARK)	Fort Valley State University	The FVSU-CDEP program has established 3+2 dual-degree programs with the University of Arkansas (UARK).
University of Detroit Mercy	Xavier University of Louisiana	The Xavier University Dual Degree Engineering Program is designed to give a solid academic background in the sciences and mathematics that are essential to persons who are interested in becoming engineers.
University of Michigan Accelerated Master's Degree Program	Spelman College	This accelerated program is designed for students to receive a bachelor's degree and Master of Science degree after five years of study.
University of Michigan - Ann Arbor	Clark Atlanta University Spelman College Morehouse College	The Dual Degree Engineering Program (DDEP) is a cooperative arrangement with the Atlanta University Center (i.e. Clark Atlanta University, Spelman College, and Morehouse College) Consortium and 15 partner engineering institutions.

Program	HBCU	Summary
University of Notre Dame	Clark Atlanta University Spelman College Morehouse College	The Dual Degree Engineering Program (DDEP) is a cooperative arrangement with the Atlanta University Center (i.e. Clark Atlanta University, Spelman College, and Morehouse College) Consortium and 15 partner engineering institutions.
University of Notre Dame	Xavier University of Louisiana	The Xavier University Dual Degree Engineering Program is designed to give a solid academic background in the sciences and mathematics that are essential to persons who are interested in becoming engineers.
University of Nevada Las Vegas	Fort Valley State University	The FVSU-CDEP program has established a 3+2 dual-degree program with the University of Nevada, Las Vegas (UNLV).
University of New Orleans	Xavier University of Louisiana	The Xavier University Dual Degree Engineering Program is designed to give a solid academic background in the sciences and mathematics that are essential to persons who are interested in becoming engineers.
University of South Carolina Darla Moore School of Business	Benedict College	The Moore School MACC Emerging Leaders Program is creating a new pathway for students from South Carolina's historically Black colleges and universities to earn Master of Accountancy degrees.
University of Southern California	Morehouse College Spelman College	Since 1969, Morehouse College has offered students the option of studying engineering through the dual-degree engineering program, which consists of cooperative agreements with a number of engineering schools.
University of Texas - Austin	Fort Valley State University	The FVSU-CDEP program has established a 3+2 dual-degree program with the University of Texas-Austin (UT-Austin).

Program	HBCU	Summary
University of Texas - Houston Biomedical Informatics Master's Degree	Tuskegee University	If students wish to further their education upon graduation from Tuskegee University, they can enroll in the McWilliams School's online master's degree program in biomedical informatics, requiring only one additional year of study. This "4+1" model will allow Tuskegee students to potentially earn a bachelor's degree, graduate certificate, and master's degree in just five years.
University of Texas Pan American (UTPA)	Fort Valley State University	The FVSU-CDEP program has established 3+2 dual-degree programs with the University of Texas Pan American (UTPA).
University of Wisconsin-Madison	Xavier University of Louisiana	The Xavier University Dual Degree Engineering Program is designed to give a solid academic background in the sciences and mathematics that are essential to persons who are interested in becoming engineers.

In Summary

The goal of what I have presented in this book is to assist students and families in being fully informed about the many opportunities available to students at HBCUs that are not available elsewhere. However, each student and family will need to weigh the option of attending an HBCU against other college options. While I have never had any of the many students with whom I have served as a college adviser express any regrets with having attending an HBCU or any of the many parents regret having their student attend an HBCU, if you watch enough videos or talk to enough students you are likely to hear that the HBCU experience was not one for everyone.

You are advised to avoid submitting an enrollment deposit to any school without visiting the campus when school is in session. Sitting in on a class whenever possible, or speaking to professors, administrators, and students. My experience is that HBCUs are welcoming campus communities where students and staff are eager to share their experiences. If you are unable to visit the campus, then I encourage you to view videos pertaining to your schools of interest on the HBCU Life TV YouTube Channel. Perhaps most important, if you apply to an HBCU or use the Black Common Application to apply to 50 or more HBCUs, develop a scholarship plan. No matter how academically accomplished you are, or great your financial need, do not sit around "hoping" that HBCUs offer you a lot of scholarship money, because it is unlikely to be forthcoming. In fact, you are more likely to have schools request an enrollment deposit BEFORE they provide you with a financial aid award letter or guarantee on-campus housing.

Visit each HBCU website, identify the cost of attendance, and assume that you will not be offered any scholarships or grants. You should begin developing your scholarship list as you enter high school. Then as a high school junior, ensure that you are prepared to apply for all of the scholarships that you identified that are only available to first-time freshmen. If you are a community college student planning to transfer to an HBCU, they begin developing a scholarship list for transfer students, or for HBCU sophomores or juniors (whichever status you have after transferring).

If you are awarded scholarships by any of the schools to which you applied, you may be able to defer some of the outside scholarships that you received until graduate school. If you are not offered any scholarships from the schools to which you applied, you might avoid student loans through the outside scholarships that you received. Either way, by being intentional and proactive, you will be better positioned to attend your top choice HBCU debt free.

* * *

Appendix: HBCU Listing

Alabama

Alabama A&M University (TMCF)
Alabama State University (TMCF)
Bishop State Community College (TMCF)
C.A. Fredd Campus of Shelton State Community College (TMCF)
Gadsden State Community College (TMCF)
H Councill Trenholm State Community College (TMCF)
J.F. Drake State Community and Technical College (TMCF)
Lawson State Community College (TMCF)
Miles College (UNCF)
Oakwood University (UNCF)
Shelton State Community College (TMCF)
Stillman College (UNCF)
Talladega College (UNCF)
Tuskegee University (TMCF)/(UNCF)

Arkansas

Arkansas Baptist College
Philander Smith University (UNCF)
Shorter College
University of Arkansas at Pine Bluff (TMCF)

California

Charles R. Drew University of Medicine & Science (TMCF)

Delaware

Delaware State University (TMCF)

District of Columbia

Howard University (TMCF)/(UNCF)
University of the District of Columbia (TMCF)
University of the District of Columbia-
David A Clarke School of Law (TMCF)

Florida

Bethune-Cookman University (UNCF)
Edward Waters College (UNCF)
Florida Agricultural and Mechanical University (TMCF)
Florida Memorial University (UNCF)

Georgia

Albany State University (TMCF)
Clark Atlanta University (UNCF)
Fort Valley State University (TMCF)
Interdenominational Theological Center (UNCF)
Morehouse College (UNCF)
Morehouse School of Medicine
Morris Brown College
Paine College (UNCF)
Savannah State University (TMCF)
Spelman College (UNCF)

Kentucky

Kentucky State University (TMCF)
Simmons College of Kentucky

Louisiana

Dillard University (UNCF)
Grambling State University (TMCF)
Southern University and A&M College (TMCF)
Southern University at New Orleans (TMCF)
Southern University at Shreveport (TMCF)
Southern University Law Center (TMCF)
Xavier University of Louisiana (UNCF)

Maryland

Bowie State University (TMCF)
Coppin State University (TMCF)
Morgan State University (TMCF)
University of Maryland Eastern Shore (TMCF)

Mississippi

Alcorn State University (TMCF)
Coahoma Community College
Jackson State University (TMCF)
Mississippi Valley State University (TMCF)
Rust College (UNCF)
Tougaloo College (UNCF)

Missouri

Harris-Stowe State University (TMCF)
Lincoln University (MO) (TMCF)

North Carolina

Bennett College (UNCF)
Elizabeth City State University (TMCF)
Fayetteville State University (TMCF)
Johnson C. Smith University (UNCF)
Livingstone College (UNCF)
North Carolina A&T State University (TMCF)
North Carolina Central University (TMCF)
Saint Augustine's University (UNCF)
Shaw University (UNCF)
Winston-Salem State University (TMCF)

Ohio

Central State University (TMCF)
Wilberforce University (UNCF)

Oklahoma

Langston University (TMCF)

Pennsylvania

Cheyney University of Pennsylvania (TMCF)
Lincoln University (PA) (TMCF)

South Carolina

Allen University (UNCF)
Benedict College (UNCF)
Claflin University (UNCF)
Clinton College
Denmark Technical College (TMCF)

Morris College (UNCF)
South Carolina State University (TMCF)
Voorhees University (UNCF)

Tennessee

American Baptist College
Fisk University (UNCF)
Lane College (UNCF)
LeMoyne-Owen College (UNCF)
Meharry Medical College
Tennessee State University (TMCF)

Texas

Huston-Tillotson University (UNCF)
Jarvis Christian College (UNCF)
Paul Quinn College
Prairie View A&M University (TMCF)
Southwestern Christian College
St. Philip's College
Texas College (UNCF)
Texas Southern University (TMCF)
Wiley University (UNCF)

U.S. Virgin Islands

University of the Virgin Islands (TMCF)

Virginia

Hampton University
Norfolk State University (TMCF)
Virginia State University (TMCF)
Virginia Union University (UNCF)
Virginia University of Lynchburg

West Virginia

Bluefield State University (TMCF)
West Virginia State University (TMCF)

References

2024 Black Students and STEM Report. (2024). From classroom to career: How interventions in middle and high school can help Black students succeed in STEM careers. You Science and Black Girls Do STEM. Retrieved 9/21/24, from https://resources.youscience.com/rs/806-BFU-539/images/2024_BlackStudentSTEM_Report.pdf?version=1

A Voice for Independent Higher Education in South Carolina. (2021). Claflin University receives $5 million STEM grant from Google. Retrieved 9/21/24, from https://scicu.org/claflin-university-receives-5-million-stem-grant-from-google/

Accenture. (2024). A Global Business Consulting Firm. Retrieved 9/21/24, from https://www.accenture.com/us-en

Accreditation Board for Engineering and Technology (ABET). (2024). Retrieved 9/21/24, from https://www.abet.org/about-abet/history/

ACT Inc. (2023). ACT Score National Ranks. Retrieved 9/21/24, from https://www.act.org/content/dam/act/unsecured/documents/MultipleChoiceStemComposite.pdf

ACT Inc. (2023). Profile Report - National: Graduating Class of 2023. Retrieved 9/21/24, from https://www.act.org/content/dam/act/unsecured/documents/2023-National-ACT-Profile-Report.pdf

Alabama A&M University. (2024). AAMU Artificial Intelligence Lab Gets Boost from Army. Retrieved 9/21/24, from https://www.aamu.edu/research-economic-development/news/aamu-ai-lab-gets-boost-from-army.html

Alcorn, C. (2021). Major companies are recruiting more HBCU grads than ever, administrators say. ABC 11 Eyewitness News. Retrieved 9/21/24, from https://abc11.com/hbcu-jobs-increase-in-hiring-of-graduates-black-americans-business-schools/10947404/

American Council on Education. (2024). Retrieved 9/21/24, from https://www.acenet.edu/Pages/default.aspx

American Council on Education. (2024). Carnegie Classification of Institutions of Higher Education. Retrieved 9/21/24, from https://carnegieclassifications.acenet.edu/carnegie-classification/

American Council on Education. (2024). Carnegie Classification of Institutions of Higher Education: 2025 Research Designations. Retrieved 9/21/24, from https://carnegieclassifications.acenet.edu/carnegie-classification/research-designations/

American Council on Education. (2024). Carnegie Classification of Institutions of Higher Education: Basic Carnegie Classifications. Retrieved 9/21/24, from https://carnegieclassifications.acenet.edu/carnegie-classification/classification-methodology/basic-classification/

American Council on Education. (2024). Carnegie Classification of Institutions of Higher Education: Institution Research. Retrieved 9/21/24, from https://carnegieclassifications.acenet.edu/institutions/?inst=&hbcu%5B%5D=1

American Institute of Physics. (2024). The Time is Now: Systemic Changes to Increase African Americans with Bachelor's Degrees in Physics and Astronomy. Retrieved 9/21/24, from https://www.aip.org/sites/default/files/aipcorp/files/teamup-full-report.pdf

Anderson, V., Burdman, P. (2022). A New Calculus for College Admissions: How Policy, Practice, and Perceptions of High School Math Education Limit Equitable Access to College. National Association of College Admissions Counseling (NACAC) and Just Equations. Retrieved 9/21/24, from https://cdn.prod.website-files.com/61afa2b5ded66610900a0b97/644aec77a5f4e9c3f54efc28_New-Calc-College-Admissions-FINAL-update-4-23.pdf

Apple Computer. (2021). Apple launches major new Racial Equity and Justice Initiative projects to challenge systemic racism, advance racial equity nationwide. Retrieved 9/21/24, from https://www.apple.com/newsroom/2021/01/apple-launches-major-new-racial-equity-and-justice-initiative-projects-to-challenge-systemic-racism-advance-racial-equity-nationwide/

Atlanta News First. (2024). Spelman College receives $100 million donation, largest in HBCU history. [Video]. YouTube. Retrieved 9/21/24, from https://youtu.be/aiVD0VAsQjI?si=WjrSpalSE28WDCmu

Aviation Accreditation Board International. (2024). Directory of Accredited Programs. Retrieved 9/21/24, from https://www.aabi.aero/accreditation/accredited-programs/

Baker, M., Morgan, I., & Wade, G. (2023). Opportunities Denied: High-Achieving Black and Latino Students Lack Access to Advanced Math. The Education Trust and Just Equations. Retrieved 9/21/24, from https://edtrust.org/wp-content/uploads/2014/09/Advanced-Math-V9.pdf

Barnett, S. (2023). 'The stars aligning': Students reflect on Tougaloo-Brown exchange semester, share advice for applicants. The Brown Daily Herald. Retrieved 9/21/24, from https://www.browndailyherald.com/article/2023/09/the-stars-aligning-students-reflect-on-tougaloo-brown-

exchange-semester-share-advice-for-applicants
Bethune-Cookman University. (2024). The NASA MUREP DEAP Institute: Research and Funding Opportunity. Retrieved 9/21/24, from https://www.cookman.edu/cnhsem/murep/index.html
BGE. (2024). BGE Celebrates Partnerships with Local HBCUs. [Video]. YouTube. Retrieved 9/21/24, from https://youtu.be/_cQlsbq0HoY?si=gKS_AyrrlVkQqz4n
Binkley, C., MA, A. (2023). Black and Latino students lack access to certified teachers and advanced classes. Associated Press. Retrieved 9/21/24, from https://apnews.com/article/black-latino-students-civil-rights-school-7203f99c430a71c90388cfcd330b5f1c
Bromley, A. (2019). UVA-Led Program Seeks to Broaden the Pool of STEM Researchers (Bennett College). University of Virginia. Retrieved 9/21/24, from https://news.virginia.edu/content/uva-led-program-seeks-broaden-pool-stem-researchers
Brown University. (2024). Brown-Tougaloo Partnership. Retrieved 9/21/24, from https://tougaloo.brown.edu/
Butrymowicz, S., Amy, J., & Fenn, L. (2020). How career and technical education shuts out Black and Latino students from high-paying professions. The Hechinger Report. Retrieved 9/21/24, from https://hechingerreport.org/how-career-and-technical-education-shuts-out-black-and-latino-students-from-high-paying-professions/
CAE in Cybersecurity. (2024). National Center for Excellence in Cybersecurity Education. National Security Agency/Department of Homeland Security. Retrieved 11/5/24, from https://caecommunity.org/about-us/what-cae-cybersecurity
Caltech. (2024). Caltech 3/2 Program. Caltech Undergraduate Admissions. Retrieved 9/21/24, from https://www.admissions.caltech.edu/apply/32-program
Career Communications Group. (2024). 2024 Top Supporters of HBCU Engineering Schools. Retrieved 9/21/24, from https://intouch.ccgmag.com/page/hbcu-top-supporters-list-2024
Carnevale, A., Rose, S., Cheah, B. (2011). The College Payoff - Education, Occupations, Lifetime Earnings. Georgetown University Center for Education and The Workforce: Washington, DC.
Center of Excellence in Cybersecurity. (2024). South Carolina State University. Retrieved 11/5/24, from https://mcs.scsu.edu/cybersecurity/
Claybourn, Cole. (2024). Attending an Online School: What to Consider. U.S. News & World Reports. Retrieved 9/21/24, from https://www.usnews.com/education/best-high-schools/articles/attending-an-online-high-school
CodeHouse Scholars. (2024). Retrieved 9/21/24, from https://www.thecodehouse.org/
Cognosante. (2024). HBCU Partner Alliance. [Video]. YouTube. Retrieved 9/21/24, from https://youtu.be/d06kZMIkgTA?si=OiSeF6aTJc3iMwTQ
CollegeBoard. (2024). AP Courses and Exams. 2024. Retrieved 9/21/24, from https://apstudents.collegeboard.org/courses
Council for Higher Education Accreditation (CHEA). (2024). Retrieved 9/21/24, from https://www.chea.org/
Crockett, J. (2023). N.C. A&T-Led Research Team Awarded NASA Grant for Flood Monitoring Data Science Research. North Carolina Agricultural and Technical State University. Retrieved 9/21/24, from https://ncat.edu/news/2023/04/nasa-deap-institute-hashemi-beni.php
Day, D. (2023). Princeton-HBCU research collaborations continue with 10 new projects. Princeton University Strategic Partnerships & Engagement Office of Innovation. Retrieved 9/21/24, from https://partnerships.princeton.edu/news/2023/princeton-hbcu-research-collaborations-continue-10-new-projects
Dillard University. (2024). Dillard University Awarded $19.94 Million Community Change Grant by Environment Protection Agency (EPA). Retrieved 9/21/24, from https://www.dillard.edu/du-news/dillard-awarded-19million-community-change-grant/
Dillard University. (2024). HBCU Clean Energy Education Prize - Dillard University. [Video]. YouTube. Retrieved 9/21/24, from https://youtu.be/KCb9ED7XZTc?si=0AS6DvRyoNSfzh67
Dillard University. (2024). Mathematics and Actuarial Science Program. Retrieved 9/21/24, from https://www.dillard.edu/programs/mathematics-actuarial-science/
Enviva. (2024). Enviva Establishes a $250,000 Endowed Scholarship for the College of Agriculture and Environmental Sciences at North Carolina Agricultural & Technical State University. Retrieved 9/21/24, from https://www.envivabiomass.com/enviva-establishes-a-250000-endowed-scholarship-for-the-college-of-agriculture-and-environmental-sciences-at-north-carolina-agricultural-technica-l-state-university/
Enviva. (2024). Leading in sustainable wood bioenergy. Retrieved 9/21/24, from https://www.envivabiomass.com/
ESG News. (2023). NASA to Award 11.7 Million to Eight Historically Black Colleges, Universities. Retrieved 9/21/24, from https://esgnews.com/nasa-to-award-11-7-million-to-eight-historically-black-colleges-universities/

Federal Aviation Administration. (2024). HBCU Initiative Group - Employee Spotlight: Alan Kiel. [Video]. YouTube. Retrieved 9/21/24, from https://youtu.be/veOz6DPM_yA?si=8v8eebpF39-ytQ4h

Federal Aviation Administration. (2024). HBCU Initiative Group - Employee Spotlight: Marcus Ward. [Video]. YouTube. Retrieved 9/21/24, from https://youtu.be/ahtl4VjX7_U?si=sNA2Fr1twUFrum4X

Federal Aviation Administration. (2024). FAA HBCU Initiative Overview. [Video]. YouTube. Retrieved 9/21/24, from https://youtu.be/oE7cE_BFs5w?si=o3pTQBvQCp3NW2BS

Federal Aviation Administration. (2024). HBCU Pride at the FAA. [Video]. YouTube. Retrieved 9/21/24, from https://youtu.be/mlxoSkyxWTE?si=E9vV79bjgQG6Scod

Fenley, N. (2022). 11 HBCUs Awarded The Coveted R2 Status in the New Carnegie Classification Update. Blavity. Retrieved 9/21/24, from https://blavity.com/10-hbcus-awarded-the-coveted-r2-status-in-the-new-carnegie-classification-update.

Floyd, J. (2022). Renewable Energy. TheGrio. Retrieved 9/21/24, from https://thegrio.com/2022/02/09/hbcus-renewable-energy/

Foundation for Ensuring Access and Equity. (2024). Student Overcomes the Odds to Receive $1.8 Million In Scholarships, Including Full Scholarships to 6 Top Colleges. Retrieved 9/21/24, from https://www.send2press.com/wire/student-overcomes-the-odds-to-receive-1-8-million-in-scholarships-including-full-scholarships-to-6-top-colleges/

Fulbright. (2024). Top Producing Institutions. Retrieved 9/21/24, from https://www.fulbrightprogram.org/tpi/

Fulbright. (2024). U.S. Department of State Recognizes 19 Historically Black Colleges and Universities in 13 States and Washington, D.C. as Fulbright HBCU Institutional Leaders. Retrieved 9/21/24, from https://www.fulbrightprogram.org/19-fulbright-hbcu-institutional-leaders/

Gallardo, S. (2024). HBCU Colleges with Veterinary Programs: A Comprehensive Guide. HBCULifestyle. Retrieved 9/21/24, from https://hbculifestyle.com/hbcu-colleges-with-veterinary-programs/

Georgia Tech. (2024). HBCU & MSI Research Collaboration Initiative. Retrieved 9/21/24, from https://research.gatech.edu/hbcu-msi

Ginther, S., et.al. (2011). Race, Ethnicity, and NIH Research Awards. National Library of Medicine National Center for Biotechnology Information. Retrieved 9/21/24, from https://www.ncbi.nlm.nih.gov/pmc/articles/PMC3412416/

GlobeNewswire. (2024). UNCF and Founding HBCUs Sign Historic Agreement to Launch HBCUv, a Digital Learning and Community Engagement Platform "By HBCUs, For HBCUs." Retrieved 9/21/24, from https://www.globenewswire.com/news-release/2024/08/08/2927206/0/en/UNCF-and-Founding-HBCUs-Sign-Historic-Agreement-to-Launch-HBCUv-a-Digital-Learning-and-Community-Engagement-Platform-By-HBCUs-For-HBCUs.html

HBCUColleges. (2024). HBCU Computer Science Schools - 2024 Ranking. Retrieved 9/21/24, from https://hbcu-colleges.com/computer

HBCUConnect.com. (2017). Dept. of Justice Awards HBCU Consortium Grant; N.C. A&T Lead Institution. Retrieved 9/21/24, from https://hbcuconnect.com/content/301069/dept-of-justice-awards-hbcu-consortium-grant-n-c-a-t-lead-institution

HBCU Battle of the Brains. (2024). Retrieved 9/21/24, from https://hbcubattleofthebrains.com/

HBCU Chips Network. (2024). Retrieved 9/21/24, from https://hbcuchips.org/

HBCU Chips Network. (2024). HBCU Research Network Map. Retrieved 9/21/24, from https://hbcuchips.org/research

History.com. (2024). The Great Migration. Retrieved 9/21/24, from https://www.history.com/topics/black-history/great-migration

IBM. (2024). A Global Business and Computing Company. Retrieved 9/21/24, from https://www.ibm.com/us-en

Howard University. (2024). Department of Mathematics Course Requirements for Applied Mathematics. Retrieved 9/21/24, from https://mathematics.howard.edu/academics/undergraduate-program

Howard University. (2024). Examining the impact of the IBM-HBCU Quantum Center. [Video]. YouTube. Retrieved 9/21/24, from https://youtu.be/9xbnb5C60BU?si=RqgFfopd4IDNWXYa.

Howard University. (2024). IBM-HBCU Quantum Center. Retrieved 9/21/24, from https://coas.howard.edu/research/research-initiatives/hbcu-quantum-howard-university

Howard University. (2024). Independent Exchange Program. Retrieved 9/21/24, from https://howard.edu/academics/exchange/huiep

Howard University. (2024). Office of Research. Retrieved 9/21/24, from https://research.howard.edu/

History.com. (2024). The Great Migration. Retrieved 9/21/24, from https://www.history.com/topics/black-history/great-migration

IBM. (2024). A Global Business and Computing Company. Retrieved 9/21/24, from https://www.ibm.com/us-en

International Game Developers Association. (2022). Developer Satisfaction Survey 2021.

Retrieved 9/21/24, from https://igda-website.s3.us-east-2.amazonaws.com/wp-content/uploads/2022/11/15161607/IGDA-DSS-2021-Diversity-Report_Final.pdf
Johnson C. Smith University. (2024). JCSU STEM Program Receives Prestigious $1 Million U.S. Department of Homeland Security Grant. Retrieved 9/21/24, from https://www.jcsu.edu/news/jcsu-stem-program-receives-prestigious-1-million-us-department-homeland-security-grant
Kennedy-King College. (2024). City Colleges of Chicago. Retrieved 9/21/24, from https://www.ccc.edu/kennedy/home/
Kentucky Science & Technology Corporation. (2024). NSF Awards $7M to Kentucky State University, Kentucky Science and Engineering Foundation and Partners for AgTech Research. Retrieved 9/21/24, from https://www.kstc.org/post/nsf-awards-7m-to-kentucky-state-university-kentucky-science-and-engineering-foundation-and-partner
Kochhar, R., & Moslimani, M. (2023). Wealth gaps across racial and ethnic groups. Pew Research Center. Retrieved 9/21/24, from https://www.pewresearch.org/2023/12/04/wealth-gaps-across-racial-and-ethnic-groups/
Lenhart, A. (2015). Chapter 3: Video Games Are Key Elements in Friendships for Many Boys. Pew Research Center. Retrieved 9/21/24, from https://www.pewresearch.org/internet/2015/08/06/chapter-3-video-games-are-key-elements-in-friendships-for-many-boys/#:~:text=While%20black%20teens%20(83%25),strategize%20and%20talk%20while%20playing.
Lopez, T. (2023). Howard University Will Be Lead Institution for New Research Center. U.S. Department of Defense. Retrieved 9/21/24, from https://www.defense.gov/News/News-Stories/Article/Article/3275321/howard-university-will-be-lead-institution-for-new-research-center/
Menzies, S., Stein. (2024). Cultivating and leveraging the community cultural wealth of Black students in high cognitive demand elementary mathematics classrooms. Teaching and Teacher Education. Retrieved 9/21/24, from https://www.sciencedirect.com/science/article/abs/pii/S0742051X24002142
Meyer, T. (2022). Princeton partners with UNCF and HBCUs to expand research and innovation. Princeton University Strategic Partnerships & Engagement Office of Innovation. Retrieved 9/21/24, from https://partnerships.princeton.edu/news/2022/princeton-partners-uncf-and-hbcus-expand-research-and-innovation
Michigan State University. (2024). The Apple Developer Academy is a partnership between MSU and Apple. Retrieved 9/21/24, from https://developeracademy.msu.edu/
Morehouse College. (2024). Summer Programs. Retrieved 9/21/24, from https://morehouse.edu/academics/programs/summer-academy
Morgan State University. (2023). Long-Term, High-Resolution Urban Aerosol Database for Research, Education and Outreach Project. Retrieved 9/21/24, from https://www.morgan.edu/ceamls/news/ceamls-lthua-press-release9/12/24.
Morgan State University. (2020). Morgan's Actuarial Science Program Aims to Diversify a Competitive Profession. Retrieved 9/21/24, from https://news.morgan.edu/actuarial-science-diversity/
NASA. (2024). NASA Awards Millions to Historically Black Colleges, Universities. Retrieved 9/21/24, from https://www.nasa.gov/news-release/nasa-awards-millions-to-historically-black-colleges-universities/
National Assessment of Educational Progress. (2022). Mathematics Assessment 2022. Retrieved 9/21/24, from https://nces.ed.gov/nationsreportcard/mathematics/
National Center for Education Statistics. (2024). Advanced mathematics and science courses (97). Retrieved 9/21/24, from https://nces.ed.gov/fastfacts/display.asp?id=97
National Center for Education Statistics. (2017). Beginning College Students Who Change Their Majors Within 3 Years of Enrollment. Retrieved 9/21/24, from https://nces.ed.gov/pubs2018/2018434/index.asp
National Center for Education Statistics. (2016). Indicator 13: High School Coursetaking. Retrieved 9/21/24, from https://nces.ed.gov/programs/raceindicators/indicator_rcd.asp
National Center for Health Workforce Analysis. (2024). State of the U.S. Health Care Workforce, 2023. Bureau of Health Workforce. Retrieved 9/21/24, from https://bhw.hrsa.gov/sites/default/files/bureau-health-workforce/data-research/state-of-the-health-workforce-report-2023.pdf
National Center for Science and Engineering Statistics. (2023). Diversity and STEM: Women, Minorities, and Persons with Disabilities. Retrieved 9/21/24, from https://ncses.nsf.gov/pubs/nsf23315/
National Merit Scholarship Corporation. (2024). National Merit Scholarship. Retrieved 9/21/24, from https://www.nationalmerit.org/s/1758/start.aspx?gid=2&pgid=61&no_cookie=1
National Nuclear Security Administration. (2024). NNSA Minority Serving Institution Partnership Program (MSIPP). Retrieved 9/21/24, from https://www.energy.gov/nnsa/nnsa-minority-serving-institution-partnership-program-msipp
National Telecommunications and Information Administration. (2024). Connecting Minority Communities

Pilot Program. Retrieved 9/21/24, from https://www.ntia.gov/funding-programs/internet-all/connecting-minority-communities-pilot-program

NBC4 Washington. (2024). Howard grad makes U. S. Air Force Thunderbird history. [Video]. YouTube. Retrieved 9/21/24, from https://youtu.be/iQK6iUzH1Mw?si=KBl4x7JH0O71nJCQ

NBC News. (2024). Texas Southern University offers aviation program to bring diversity to field. [Video]. YouTube. Retrieved 9/21/24, from https://youtu.be/d7jYALvYwgE?si=fKmSuRqr20nLW1qX

News 19 WLTX. (2024). IBM Partnering with HBCUs. [Video]. YouTube. Retrieved 9/21/24, from https://youtu.be/JXXFELG0Mvo?si=gyJcstlflvWA2YiG

Newsome, M. (2021). Even as colleges pledge to improve, share of engineering and math graduates who are Black declines. The Hechinger Report. Retrieved 9/21/24, from https://hechingerreport.org/even-as-colleges-pledge-to-improve-share-of-engineering-graduates-who-are-black-declines/

NewsOne Now. Intel Invests $4.5 Million Into HBCU STEM Programs At Six Universities. [Video]. YouTube. Retrieved 9/21/24, from https://youtu.be/ngtUNtbhj5k?si=OUIDCOX8wrRJM1xA

North Carolina A&T State University. (2024). Department of Family and Consumer Sciences Curriculum for Food and Nutritional Scientists. Retrieved 9/21/24, from https://ncat.edu/provost/academic-affairs/curriculum-guides/2019-2020/CAES/fall-2019-food-science-curriculum-guide.pdf

Northeastern University. (2024). College of Engineering. Retrieved 9/21/24, from https://coe.northeastern.edu/

Northeastern University. (2024). Cooperative Education. Retrieved 9/21/24, from https://experiential-learning.northeastern.edu/coop/

Oak Ridge National Laboratory. (2024). Fostering Strategic Partnerships with HBCUs and HSIs. [Video]. YouTube. Retrieved 9/21/24, from https://youtu.be/HbjPDwcQ16Y?si=qTRSON8p2lx3uRSu

Patrick, K., Davis, J., & Socol, A.R. (2022). Why Are Black and Latino Students Shut Out of AP STEM Courses? Ed Trust. Retrieved 9/21/24, from https://edtrust.org/resource/why-are-black-and-latino-students-shut-out-of-ap-stem-courses/

Pearson, T. (2020). Why the most lucrative tech careers are still out of reach for so many US students. Quartz. Retrieved 9/21/24, from https://qz.com/1945141/5-ways-to-get-more-us-students-of-color-into-computer-science

Peebles, J. (2023). 6 HBCUs Offering Summer Programs. HBCUBuzz. Retrieved 9/21/24, from https://hbcubuzz.com/2023/06/6-hbcus-offering-summer-programs/

Plaut, A. (2024). Top 10 HBCUs for Computer Science Programs. BestColleges. Retrieved 9/21/24, from https://www.bestcolleges.com/computer-science/top-hbcus/

PR Newswire. (2023). BP Invests in Future Talent with HBCU Fellowship Program. Retrieved 9/21/24, from https://www.prnewswire.com/news-releases/bp-invests-in-future-talent-with-hbcu-fellowship-program-301750266.html

Prairie View A&M University. (2023). Making History: PVAMU launched $40M national University Transportation Center. Retrieved 9/21/24, from https://www.pvamu.edu/research/post/making-history-pvamu-launched-40m-national-university-transportation-center/

Prairie View A&M University. (2024). Prairie View A&M University's Engineering Department Receives $160,000 NSF Grant for Artificial Intelligence STEM Research. Retrieved 9/21/24, from https://www.pvamu.edu/research/post/prairie-view-am-universitys-engineering-department-receives-160000-nsf-grant-for-artificial-intelligence-stem-research/

Propel. (2024). HBCU Cybersecurity Accelerator. Retrieved 9/21/24, from https://propelcenter.org/hbcucybersecurityaccelerator

Propel. (2024). Pioneering Health Accelerator. Retrieved 9/21/24, from https://propelcenter.org/pioneeringhealthaccelerator

Race and Ethnicity in Higher Education. (2020). Race and Ethnicity in Higher Education: 2020 Supplement. Retrieved 9/21/24, from https://www.equityinhighered.org/resources/report-downloads/race-and-ethnicity-in-higher-education-a-status-report/

Rankins MD, C. (2020). Historically Black Colleges and Universities (HBCUs): NSF's Role in Building Capacity for STEM Education and Research. National Science Foundation. Retrieved 9/21/24, from https://www.nsf.gov/nsb/meetings/2020/0729/presentations/Plenary-Open-HBCU.pdf

Riddick, J. (2024). Good News in the Progress Toward Top-Tier Research Status for HBCUs? Center for Security and Emerging Technology. Retrieved 9/21/24, from https://cset.georgetown.edu/article/good-news-in-the-progress-toward-top-tier-research-status-for-hbcus/

Scienticamerican.com. (2021). Modern Mathematics Confronts Its White, Patriarchal Past. Retrieved 9/21/24, from https://www.scientificamerican.com/article/modern-mathematics-confronts-its-white-patriarchal-past/

Shepard, Q. (2023). NCCU receives $1.4 million, three-year grant from NASA. North Carolina Central University. Retrieved 9/21/24, from https://www.nccu.edu/news/nccu-receives-14-million-three-year-grant-nasa

Smith, D. (2021). Achieving Financial Equity and Justice for HBCUs. The Century Foundation. Retrieved 9/21/24, from https://tcf.org/content/report/achieving-financial-equity-justice-hbcus/
STEMUS. (2024). HBCU STEM Undergraduate Success Research Center. Retrieved 9/21/24, from https://stemuscenter.org/
South Carolina State University. (2024). Center of Excellence in Cybersecurity. Retrieved 9/21/24, from https://mcs.scsu.edu/cybersecurity/
South Carolina State University. (2024). Cybersecurity Curriculum in Computer Science. Retrieved 9/21/24, from https://scsu.edu/academics/departments/computer-science-and-mathematics/center_excellence_cybersecurity/cybersecurity_curriculum.php
Spelman College. (2024). 2023 HBCU Game Jam. [Video]. YouTube. Retrieved 9/21/24, from https://youtu.be/qGkI750EEZo?si=PrlnKCwcUAIexW6Z
Spelman College. (2024). Domestic Exchange for Spelman College Students. Retrieved 9/21/24, from https://dev4.spelman.edu/academics/office-of-the-provost/office-of-undergraduate-studies/exchange-programs/domestic-exchange
Spelman College. (2024). Spelman College Receives $200,000 Grant From the Deloitte Foundation to Support Students Pursuing STEM Fields. Retrieved 9/21/24, from https://www.spelman.edu/news/2023/07/spelman-college-receives-200,000-grant-from-the-deloitte-foundation-to-support-students-pursuing-stem-fields.html
Spelman College. (2024). Summer Programs. Retrieved 9/21/24, from https://www.spelman.edu/academics/summer-programs/
Stanford University. (2024). Stanford-HBCU Exchange Program. Retrieved 9/21/24, from https://bcsc.stanford.edu/programs/stanford-hbcu-exchange-program
STEM Learning Academic Accreditation Council (SLAAC). (2024). Retrieved 9/21/24, from https://slaac.org/about/
Strada Education Foundation. (2024). Strengthens Partnerships with SUNO to Nurture Future Leaders. [Video]. YouTube. Retrieved 9/21/24, from https://youtu.be/h5qKRiCTd1I?si=wcJ5LMN56CG4uUJr
Swayne, M. (2022) 7 Highest Paying Quantum Computer Jobs [+Average Salary]. Quantum Insider. Retrieved 11/5/24, from https://thequantuminsider.com/2022/04/20/top-quantum-computing-jobs-for-workers-in-emerging-quantum-fields/
Temming, M. (2021). STEM's racial, ethnic and gender gaps are still strikingly large. ScienceNews. Retrieved 9/21/24, from https://www.scientificamerican.com/article/modern-mathematics-confronts-its-white-patriarchal-past/
Tennessee State University. (2024). HBCU Clean Energy Education Prize - Tennessee State University. [Video]. YouTube. Retrieved 9/21/24, from https://youtu.be/myLfZp3_22I?si=Yvuzr_ZwEx7vkPmg
Tuskegee University. (2024). Distinguished Presidential Scholarship. Retrieved 9/21/24, from https://www.tuskegee.edu/programs-courses/scholarships/freshman-scholarships
Tuskegee University. (2024). Mechanical Engineering Curriculum. Retrieved 9/21/24, from https://www.tuskegee.edu/programs-courses/colleges-schools/coe/mechanical-engineering/curriculum
Tuskegee University. (2024). Summer Programs. Retrieved 9/21/24, from https://www.tuskegee.edu/research-innovation/summer-programs
U.S. Black Engineer Information Technology. (2023). Updated: Explore STEM Summer Camps and Programs at HBCUs. Retrieved 9/21/24, from https://www.blackengineer.com/imported_wordpress/updated-explore-stem-summer-camps-programs-hbcus-mp-1/
U.S. Bureau of Labor Statistics. (2024). Occupational Outlook Handbook: Architecture and Engineering Occupations. Retrieved 9/21/24, from https://www.bls.gov/ooh/Architecture-and-Engineering/
U.S. Bureau of Labor Statistics. (2024). Occupational Outlook Handbook: Computer and Information Technology Occupations. Retrieved 9/21/24, from https://www.bls.gov/ooh/computer-and-information-technology/home.htm
U.S. Bureau of Labor Statistics. (2024). Occupational Outlook Handbook: Fastest Growing Occupations. Retrieved 9/21/24, from https://www.bls.gov/ooh/fastest-growing.htm
U.S. Bureau of Labor Statistics. (2024). Occupational Outlook Handbook: Math Occupations. Retrieved 9/21/24, from https://www.bls.gov/ooh/math/home.htm
U.S. Bureau of Labor Statistics. (2024). Occupational Outlook Handbook: Life, Physical, and Social Science Occupations. Retrieved 9/21/24, from https://www.bls.gov/ooh/life-physical-and-social-science/home.htm
U.S. Department of Commerce. (2024). Biden-Harris Administration Announces Over $5 Billion from the CHIPS and Science Act for Research, Development, and Workforce. Retrieved 9/21/24, from https://www.commerce.gov/news/fact-sheets/2024/02/fact-sheet-biden-harris-administration-announces-over-5-billion-chips-and
U.S. Department of Defense. (2024). DoD HBCU/MI Internship: An Important Opportunity. [Video]. YouTube. Retrieved 9/21/24, from https://youtu.be/RRTatLJa5Yc?si=ybKcxP6BV312FVCa

U.S. Department of Education. (2023). Secretaries of Education, Agriculture Call on Governors to Equitably Fund Land-Grant HBCUs. Retrieved 9/21/24, from https://www.ed.gov/news/press-releases/secretaries-education-agriculture-call-governors-equitably-fund-land-grant-hbcus
U.S. Department of Education. (2024). Biden-Harris Administration Announces Record Over $16 Billion in Support for Historically Black Colleges and Universities (HBCUs). Retrieved 9/21/24, from https://www.ed.gov/news/press-releases/fact-sheet-biden-%E2%81%A0harris-administration-announces-record-over-16-billion-support-historically-black-colleges-and-universities-hbcus
U.S. Department of Energy. (2023). U.S. Department of Energy Announces $37 Million to Build Research Capacity at Historically Underrepresented Institutions. Retrieved 9/21/24, from https://www.energy.gov/articles/us-department-energy-announces-37-million-build-research-capacity-historically
U.S. Department of Transportation. (2023). U.S. Department of Transportation Funds Innovative Research Providing Vital Training for Next Generation of Transportation Leaders. Retrieved 9/21/24, from https://www.transportation.gov/briefing-room/us-department-transportation-funds-innovative-research-providing-vital-training-next
U.S. National Science Foundation. (2024). Graduate Research Fellowship Program. Retrieved 9/21/24, from https://www.nsfgrfp.org/
U.S. Navy. (2024). Office of Naval Research: Department of Navy's HBCU/MI Program. Retrieved 9/21/24, from https://www.onr.navy.mil/hbcu
U.S. Navy. (2024). Office of Naval Research: Naval STEM. Retrieved 9/21/24, from https://www.onr.navy.mil/education-outreach/naval-stem
U.S. News. (2024). U.S. News & World Reports Best National University Rankings. Retrieved 9/21/24, from https://www.usnews.com/best-colleges/rankings/national-universities
Unigo. (2024). BRPH Future Achievers Scholarship. Retrieved 9/21/24, from https://www.myscholarship.app/brph
United Airlines. (2024). United - Hampton University pilots inspiring future aviators to soar. [Video]. YouTube. Retrieved 9/21/24, from https://youtu.be/mncC1kYqiaY?si=hP6hhPx6w6xX04Be
United Negro College Fund. (2024). Dillard University Receives $1.25 Million for STEM Education and Research. Retrieved 9/21/24, from https://uncf.org/the-latest/dillard-university-receives-1-25-million-for-stem-education-and-research
United Negro College Fund. (2024). The Impact of HBCUs on Diversity in STEM Fields. Retrieved 9/21/24, from https://uncf.org/the-latest/the-impact-of-hbcus-on-diversity-in-stem-fields
United Negro College Fund. (2023). UNCF and Google are Paving the Path Forward to Increase Opportunities for HBCU Students in Tech Fields with Additional $2M Investment (Morehouse and NC A&T). Retrieved 9/21/24, from https://uncf.org/news/uncf-and-google-are-paving-the-path-forward-to-increase-opportunities-for-hbcu-students-in-tech-fields-with-additional-2m-investment
University of California. (2024). Statement on Mathematics - BOARS Area C Workgroup Stage 1 Report. Retrieved 9/21/24, from https://senate.universityofcalifornia.edu/_files/committees/boars/documents/boarsacwphase1report-20240221.pdf
University of Mississippi News. (2021). School of Engineering, Rust College Partner for Dual-Degree Program. Retrieved 9/21/24, from https://news.olemiss.edu/school-of-engineering-rust-college-partner-for-dual-degree-program/
WBBJ 7 Eyewitness News. (2020). Lane College announces grant from National Science Foundation. Retrieved 9/21/24, from https://www.wbbjtv.com/2020/10/29/lane-college-announces-grant-from-national-science-foundation/
Weissman, S. (2022). Striving for the 'Gold Standard.' Inside Higher Ed. Retrieved 9/21/24, from https://www.insidehighered.com/news/2022/11/02/some-hbcus-strive-r-1-status-record-research-dollars.
WFAA News. (2024). Southwest Airlines partners with Texas HBCU to recruit future Black pilots. [Video]. YouTube. Retrieved 9/21/24, from https://youtu.be/mdUkgDZ31po?si=DjPH2Gc0iVXFXdNI
Wondwossen, W. (2020). The science behind HBCU success | NSF. National Science Foundation. Retrieved 9/21/24, from https://new.nsf.gov/science-matters/science-behind-hbcu-success
WJTV 12 News. (2024). Jackson State joins Google's HBCU career readiness program. [Video]. YouTube. Retrieved 9/21/24, from https://youtu.be/Bb67eCh5BqY?si=QTjc9O1KzkdYBLqh
Xavier University of Louisiana. (2024). Dual Degree Program in Engineering. Retrieved 9/21/24, from https://www.xula.edu/cpsc/index.html
Xavier University of Louisiana. (2024). Pre-College Programs. Retrieved 9/21/24, from https://www.xula.edu/pre-college-programs/index.html
Xavier University of Louisiana. (2024). Xavier University of Louisiana - Baylor College of Medicine BS/MD Program. Retrieved 9/21/24, from https://www.xula.edu/premed/baylorbs_md4.pdf
Xavier University of Louisiana. (2024). Xavier University of Louisiana - USC Early Assurance Program. Retrieved 9/21/24, from https://pt.usc.edu/about/diversity-anti-racism/#assurance-program
Yale University. (2024). Alliance for Scholarship, Collaboration, Engagement, Networking, and

Development ASCEND Initiative. Yale University Faculty Development & Diversity. Retrieved 9/21/24, from https://faculty.yale.edu/diversity/ascend-initiative

Footnotes

1. U.S. Bureau of Labor Statistics. (2024). Occupational Outlook Handbook: Life, Physical, and Social Science Occupations. Retrieved 9/21/24, from https://www.bls.gov/ooh/life-physical-and-social-science/home.htm
2. U.S. Bureau of Labor Statistics. (2024). Occupational Outlook Handbook: Computer and Information Technology Occupations. Retrieved 9/21/24, from https://www.bls.gov/ooh/computer-and-information-technology/home.htm
3. U.S. Bureau of Labor Statistics. (2024). Occupational Outlook Handbook: Architecture and Engineering Occupations. Retrieved 9/21/24, from https://www.bls.gov/ooh/architecture-and-engineering/home.htm
4. U.S. Bureau of Labor Statistics. (2024). Occupational Outlook Handbook: Math Occupations. Retrieved 9/21/24, from https://www.bls.gov/ooh/math/home.htm

Tables

Index

D

E

F

T

U

V

W

X

Y

www.ingramcontent.com/pod-product-compliance
Lightning Source LLC
LaVergne TN
LVHW021140160826
845679LV00023B/1986

* 9 7 8 1 8 8 0 4 6 3 5 7 4 *